Walking Washington's Gardens

A guide to 30 of the best gardens in
Washington State that are open to the public
(updated version)

Angie Narus

Walking
    Washington
    BOOKS

ISBN: 978-0-692-24778-5

My mother and me in December 2013, a few months before she was diagnosed with stage 4 cancer. She passed away in December, 2014.

This book is dedicated to my parents, Lou and Clemie, who were married for more than 60 years. Over the years, I watched them enhance the one-acre property where I grew up in Southwestern Pennsylvania. Our house was always surrounded by flower beds, and over the years my parents added a grapevine-covered arbor, benches, a pond and fountain, and vegetable garden. They sparked a love of gardening in me, and I am grateful I could share my first book with them.

May this book inspire you!

Angie Narus

Acknowledgements

I could not have written this book without assistance from the following individuals:

More than 60 people, including garden and city park directors, garden managers, head gardeners, horticulturists and other garden staff, garden volunteers, board members, and officers of garden foundations and societies helped me compile the information for this book through interviews, tours, and email correspondence. Their knowledge, input, and enthusiasm were vital to the book's content.

Special thanks to Professor John Albers of Albers Vista Gardens for his guidance and assistance, and to David Perry for providing the cover photo.

Some of my family members assisted me with editing. Their encouragement and prayers helped me stay focused. My friends were equally encouraging.

My husband enjoys touring gardens as much as I do, and he willingly went with me to visit gardens all over the state. When I told him my idea to write this book, his response of "Hmm. That's not a bad idea," got the ball rolling. Without his support, this journey would not have been nearly as much fun.

I am thankful to God for guiding me through this process.

Contents

GARDENS	Acres	Admission Fee/Suggested Donation	Open Year-Round	Guided Tours Offered	Visitor/Information Center	Gift Shop/Garden Store	Walking/Hiking Trails	Dogs Allowed On-leash
Albers Vista Gardens	4.2	•		R •				
Bellevue Botanical Garden	53	•	•	•				
Bloedel Reserve	150		•	•	•	•		
Carl S. English, Jr. Botanical Garden	7		•	•	•	•		
Center for Urban Horticulture	90		•	•	•			
Chase Garden	4.5	•		•				•
Dunn Gardens	7.5	•		R •				
Elisabeth C. Miller Botanical Garden	3			R •				
Evergreen Arboretum & Gardens	3.5	•	•	•				•
Highline SeaTac Botanical Garden	11.5		•	•				•
Hulda Klager Lilac Gardens	4.5	•	•			•		
Kubota Garden	20		•	•			•	•
Kruckeberg Botanic Garden	4	•	•	•	•			•
Lake Wilderness Arboretum	42		•	•			•	•
Lakewold Gardens	10	•	•	•		•		

Gardens marked with "R" require reservations for all visits

GARDENS	Acres	Admission Fee/Suggested Donation	Open Year-Round	Guided Tours Offered	Visitor/Information Center	Gift Shop/Garden Store	Walking/Hiking Trails	Dogs Allowed On-leash
Lawson Gardens	13		•					•
Manito Park & Gardens	90		•				•	•
Meerkerk Gardens	53	•		•		•		
Ohme Gardens	9	•						
Old Goat Farm	3		•	•		•		•
Point Defiance Park & Gardens (10 acres of gardens)	765	•	•	•			•	•
PowellsWood	3	•		•	•			
Rhododendron Species Botanical Garden	22	•	•	•		•		•
Seattle Chinese Garden	5	•	•	•				
Seattle Japanese Garden	3.5	•		•		•	•	
Soos Creek Botanical Garden	23	•	•		•			
South Seattle College Arboretum	5		•					
Volunteer Park Conservatory	---	•	•	•				
Washington Park Arboretum	230	•	•	•			•	•
W.W. Seymour Conservatory	---	•	•	•		•		•
Yakima Area Arboretum	46	•	•	•			•	•

Prentice and Virginia Bloedel (sister of Eulalie Wagner of Lakewold Gardens). Mr. and Mrs. Bloedel later acquired land adjacent to the property, increasing their estate to 150 acres.

Mr. Bloedel was the owner of the MacMillan Bloedel Timber Company. He was the first to replant logged areas and develop methods of using renewable resources, including the use of sawdust to fuel his sawmills. He also demonstrated an understanding of the relationship between people and nature to a degree that seemed ahead of his time. Shorty after purchasing the Bainbridge Island property, Mr. Bloedel retired from the timber business and began focusing on developing his family's estate garden.

Mr. Bloedel's vision for the property was to display flowers, plants, and trees in a natural setting. He incorporated ideas from landscape architects Thomas Church (the contributing designer of Lakewold Gardens) and Richard Haag (the designer of Gas Works Park in Seattle) into his own plans and designed garden areas with almost seamless transitions between them. He lined woodland paths with a large collection of hardy cyclamen, orchids, trilliums, hellebores, rhododendrons, hydrangeas, and camellias, and planted candelabra primroses by the *Christmas Pond* he made for Mrs. Bloedel. One path meanders through a meadow where Mr. Bloedel grazed sheet, past a *bird marsh,* across a trestle bridge above a ravine, and along a boardwalk that crosses a

The Bloedel Reserve Visitor Center was formerly the Bloedel residence.

The Moss Garden (top left), Japanese Garden (bottom left), and Camellia Walk (above). Top left photo by Korum Bischoff.

bog of carnivorous plants. Other paths take visitors to a *Waterfall Overlook,* through a *Birch Grove* and *Rhododendron Glen,* along rows of giant camellias on the *Camellia Walk,* and past a 200-foot-long *Reflecting Pool.* There are number of paths that cross through the garden. Visitors can choose which direction to go, giving them more than one way to enjoy the garden.

Fujitaro Kubota (designer of the Kubota Garden and several gardens on the Seattle University campus) designed the Bloedel Reserve's *Japanese Garden.* His design included Japanese maples, pines, a Korean dogwood, lace leaf maples, native plants, a serene pond, and paths to create a peaceful stroll garden. The Japanese Garden Guest House, designed by architect Paul H. Kirk (designer of the Shorts House at the Bellevue Botanical Garden) combines the styles of a Japanese teahouse and a Northwest longhouse. A *Sand and Stone Garden* was later added to an outdoor space beside the guest house. Mr. Bloedel also transformed a wooded area near the Japanese Garden into a *Moss Garden*. A stream flows through a carpet of moss that is dotted with skunk cabbage, ferns, and moss-covered logs, making the garden resemble a Pacific Northwest rainforest floor.

The Bloedel family's residence was converted into a *Visitor Center,* and its original architecture, oak floors, and French stairwell were preserved. Visitors can enjoy the living room, dining room, foyer, portraits, historical exhibit, and rotating art display that provide a look into the Bloedel Reserve's past. Visitors can also peruse the Visitor Center library's collection of more than 1,400 books on horticulture topics. The east lawn is a great place to catch frequent eagle sightings and breathtaking views of Port Madison and the Cascade Mountains. The English-garden landscape between the Visitor Center and Japanese Garden is a stark contrast from the surrounding forest and other parts of the reserve. It is a mesmerizing scene with a large pond encompassed by grass lawns, a large weeping willow, Japanese maples, a Persian ironwood, and banks of heather and other flowering shrubs.

The Bloedel Reserve's mission is "to enrich people's lives through a premier public garden of natural and designed Pacific Northwest landscapes" *(the Bloedel Reserve website, 2014)*. Annual summer concerts, a summer Garden Party, a Holiday Village display, educational programs, and lectures are offered for the public. General visits do not require reservations. Public, guided walks are held seasonally and require registration, as do some of the special events. Private tours can be arranged for groups by calling (206) 842-7631. Visit the Bloedel Reserve website for more information.

DIRECTIONS FROM THE BAINBRIDGE ISLAND FERRY TERMINAL: Take SR 305 north for approximately 10 minutes to Agatewood Rd. (one road past Port Madison Rd.). Turn right on Agatewood Rd., which becomes Dolphin Drive. Follow Dolphin Drive for about one-quarter mile to the Reserve's entrance.

FROM SR 305: Go east on SR 305 through Poulsbo. Cross the Agate Pass Bridge, then turn left on Agatewood Rd. (the second road past the bridge). Agatewood Rd. becomes Dolphin Drive. Follow Dolphin Drive for about one-quarter mile to the Reserve's entrance.

Bloedel Reserve

www.bloedelreserve.org

Open Tuesday through Sunday, 10am-4pm, year-round
(Extended hours until 6pm Thursday through Sunday in
June, July, and August)

- 150 acres
- Admission fee
- General picnicking not currently permitted
- Restrooms available
- GIFT SHOP: Located in the Gate House
- STRUCTURES/FEATURES: Visitor Center in the former Bloedel House (French stairwell, oak floors, artwork, historical exhibit, rotating art display, and library), Japanese Guest House, sheep sheds, old barn, ponds, bird marsh, reflecting pool, trestle bridge, boardwalk, waterfall overlook, benches
- FEATURED PLANTS/COLLECTIONS: Japanese maples, candelabra primroses, woodland plants, ground covers, camellias, azaleas, rhododendrons, hydrangeas, trilliums, hellebores, a large collection of hardy cyclamen, Persian ironwood, Korean dogwood, weeping willow, unique trees, carnivorous plants
- ACTIVITIES: Indoor and outdoor musical performances; annual Garden Party, Founder's Weekend, and Holiday Village; art exhibits, lectures, workshops on horticulture topics, craft classes
- TOURS: Self-guided tours are welcome and do not require reservations. Public guided walks are offered seasonally, and private tours can be arranged for groups by calling (206) 842-7631. Guided walks and private tours require registration.
- NEARBY ATTRACTIONS: *On Bainbridge Island*—downtown Winslow (art galleries, art museum, history museum, waterfront park, restaurants, shopping), Fay Bainbridge Park and Beach (on Sunrise Drive), and Fort Ward Park (on Pleasant Beach Rd.); *Poulsbo*—Scandinavian-themed storefronts, restaurants, marina, waterfront park and Audubon birding trail, kayak and paddleboard rentals, Marine Science Center and Aquarium (near the marina and waterfront park)
- NEARBY GARDENS: Albers Vista Gardens; Heronswood (formal garden undergoing restoration at 7530 NE 288th St., Kingston; see *www.heronswood.com*)

Benches along the paths at Albers Vista Gardens offer resting places with views of the Port Washington Narrows.

2   Albers Vista Gardens
"An oasis in the city"

Located in a residential neighborhood in East Bremerton, West Puget Sound

124 NE 31st St.
Bremerton, WA 98310
www.albersvistagardens.org

Albers Vista Gardens is a botanic tapestry of 4.2 acres in Kitsap County. The garden was created by John Albers and Santica Marcovina, research professors of medicine at the University of Washington. Professors Albers and Marcovina purchased the property in 1998 after they saw it while touring the Olympic Peninsula. At that time, it was a mere acre of grass and fruit trees with a maple and madrone woodland overlooking the Port Washington Narrows. Professors Albers and Marcovina later purchased adjacent land overgrown with blackberry vines and scotch broom. Guided by the knowledge Professor Albers gained from horticulture classes, hands-on experience from gardening on properties he previously owned, and observing landscapes, the couple transformed the hillside. Their hard work, along with Professor Marcovina's sense of color and design, resulted in a beautiful, sustainable garden that combines native and non-native plants and trees.

Professor Albers started by laying a path of granite stepping stones to create distinct garden areas. He planted conifers in key locations to give the garden structure, then gradually integrated other plants by their characteristics and suitability for each area. More than 1,200 native species and cultivars now fill the garden, including a collection of 350 conifer cultivars such as Japanese cedars, dwarf conifers, and the rare *Abies nebrodensis* 'Sicilian Gold (Sicilian fir).'

The 14 garden rooms in this hillside oasis are as diverse as the plants they display. The planted areas are ornamented with sculptures, ceramic pots, benches, birdbaths, and whimsical features. Some of the old fruit trees remain in the garden and continue to bear fruit for the Albers family.

This view, looking down on the Three Islands and Lentz Garden, shows the depth of layers in this hillside oasis.

Left to right: The Biofiltration Garden, Santica's Perfect Solitude, and the Pollination Pathway were thoughtfully designed.

A mat of woolly thyme and other ground covers soften the stepping-stone path as it weaves its way through rhododendrons and Japanese maples, under a canopy of dawn redwoods and other evergreens in the lower *Lentz Garden*.

    The path continues up the hillside, winding through a series of other areas including memorial gardens, the Asian-inspired *Three Islands,* the *Biofiltration Garden* featuring sunroses and other drought-tolerant plants, the *Stroll Gallery* of unique trees and shrubs, a *Shade Garden* designed by Professor Marcovina, *Sam's Conifer Reserve* of dwarf conifers, *Santica's Perfect Solitude,* a restoration area, and the bordering woodland. *Santica's Perfect Solitude* showcases climbing, English, floribunda, hybrid, tea, and shrub roses high on the hillside, surrounding an elegant gazebo that offers a panoramic view of Mt. Rainier and the Port Washington Narrows. Professor Albers' book, *Gardening for Sustainability: Albers Vista Gardens of Kitsap,* gives a detailed look into this peaceful garden and its development. The book is available on the Albers Vista Gardens website.

    In 2007, the Albers Vista Gardens Foundation of Kitsap was formed to preserve, enhance, and display in perpetuity a collection of unique and botanically diverse plants in the garden using sustainable, pesticide-free gardening practices. The foundation offers opportunities for horticultural research and education at the garden, and its policies are governed by a Board of Directors made up of professionals in horticulture, landscape design, and land management.

Albers Vista Gardens can be visited through the garden's scheduled tours offered April through October, and by appointment. Requests for private group tours can be made at *info@albersvistagardens.org*. See the Albers Vista Gardens website for information on tours and special events.

DIRECTIONS FROM SR 3 (Southbound toward Bremerton): Take the Kitsap Way/SR 310 Exit in Bremerton. Go east through Bremerton. Bear left onto 11st St., then turn left onto Warren Ave./SR 303. Cross the Warren Ave. Bridge. Turn left onto Sheridan Rd. after crossing the bridge. At the bottom of the hill, turn right onto Tracyton Beach Rd., then right onto NE 31st St. Look for the black iron gate and the sign for Albers Vista Gardens about halfway up 31st St., on the left.

FROM BELFAIR OR PORT ORCHARD (Northbound on SR 3): Take SR 304 off of SR 3. Go past the shipyard, bear right (stay on 304), then turn left onto SR 303/Warren Ave. Cross the Warren Ave. Bridge. Turn left onto Sheridan Rd. after crossing the bridge. At the bottom of the hill, turn right onto Tracyton Beach Rd., then right onto NE 31st St. Look for the black iron gate and the sign for Albers Vista Gardens about halfway up 31st St., on the left.

FROM THE BREMERTON FERRY TERMINAL: Make a left onto one of the first few streets along Washington Ave. near the Bremerton waterfront and ferry terminal. Go a few blocks, then turn right onto Warren Ave. Cross the Warren Ave. Bridge. Turn left onto Sheridan Rd. after crossing the bridge. At the bottom of the hill, turn right onto Tracyton Beach Rd., then right onto NE 31st St. Look for the black iron gate and the sign for Albers Vista Gardens about halfway up 31st St., on the left.

NOTE: If your route takes you south on SR 3/SR 16 toward Tacoma or I-5, there is a toll in the southbound lanes of the Tacoma Narrows Bridge on SR 16, north of Tacoma

Albers Vista Gardens
www.albersvistagardens.org

Can be visited through scheduled tours, special events, and by appointment. Tours are offered April through October.
Reservations are required for all visits

- 4.2 acres
- Suggested donation for admission
- Restrooms available
- STRUCTURES/FEATURES: Private residence, sculptures, whimsical art, pottery, woolly thyme growing between granite stepping stones, birdbaths, gazebo, stone lanterns, benches
- FEATURED PLANTS/COLLECTIONS: Hundreds of different conifers (including dwarf conifers and weeping evergreens), maples, dawn redwoods, trees from around the world, viburnums, rhododendrons, roses, sunroses, lavender, ornamental grasses, heaths and heathers, native plants, drought-tolerant plants, plants for pollinators, ground covers
- ACTIVITIES: Educational events during summer months (usually May through September), volunteer opportunities
- TOURS: Guided tours only. Tours are offered monthly April through October on scheduled dates. Private group tours can be arranged by contacting *info@albersvistagardens.org*.
- NEARBY ATTRACTIONS: *Bremerton*—Lions Park (left on Tracyton Beach Rd. as you leave Albers Vista Gardens), Illahee State Park (trails, beach, camping); Bremerton marina (boardwalk, restaurants, ferry terminal, Navy Museum, USS Turner Joy museum); *Silverdale*— (north of Bremerton on SR 3) mall, waterfront park and public marina (playground, restrooms, small beach, pier, kayak/paddleboard rentals); *Port Orchard*—waterfront park and boardwalk, marina, waterfront shopping, public library, Sidney Art Gallery and Museum, Saturday Farmers' Market, foot ferry between Bremerton and Port Orchard
- NEARBY GARDENS: Bloedel Reserve, Anna Smith Children's Park (north of Albers Vista Gardens at 7601 Tracyton Blvd, 6.6 acres, trails, demonstration garden, butterfly house, *www.kitsapgov.com*), Elandan Gardens (outdoor bonsai display garden and specialty store, south on SR 16 between Bremerton and Port Orchard)

One of the beautifully designed borders at Point Defiance Park

3 Point Defiance Park & Gardens
"Tacoma's treasure"

Located in Tacoma's Point Defiance Park, in north Tacoma

5400 Pearl St.
Tacoma, WA 98407
www.metroparkstacoma.org

Point Defiance Park and Gardens are a significant part of
Tacoma history and beloved by local citizens. The gardens are
owned by the City of Tacoma and managed by a partnership
between Metro Parks and local gardening clubs, societies,
and other volunteers.

 The park contains eight theme gardens that have been
creatively designed and are tended by local garden groups.
The 10 acres of gardens include the *Rose Garden, Dahlia Tri-
al Garden, Rhododendron Garden, Fuchsia Garden, Herb
Garden, Iris Garden, Native Plant Garden and Meadow,* and
Japanese Garden. In the late 1800s, park superintendent

The Iris Garden and Rose Garden

Ebenezer Roberts planted the park's first *Rose Garden* with cuttings local school children had gathered for him. Now, more than an acre of rose gardens showcase over 1,500 miniature and climbing roses that are planted and maintained by the Tacoma Rose Society and volunteers. The roses peak in mid-summer.

The park's *Japanese Garden* was built in 1914 as the setting for a pagoda-style streetcar station that is now used for events. The lower part of the Japanese Garden features a pond, foot bridge, dirt path, and teahouse. The upper garden consists of a central pond adorned with a Torii Gate and Shinto Shrine given to the park by Tacoma's sister city, Kitakyushu, Japan. The pond's banks are covered with Japanese maples, azaleas, uniquely pruned pines, and shrubs. There are plans to renovate the Japanese Garden in the near future.

The five-acre *Rhododendron Garden* was established in 1956 by the American Rhododendron Society. It displays approximately 500 rhododendrons and 170 azaleas in a forest setting. Late spring is the best time to see the blooms at their finest.

The *Dahlia Trial Garden* was started in 1958 by the Washington State Dahlia Society. It is one of the largest official test gardens in the U.S. and Canada for determining which dahlia varieties will be sold commercially. The dahlias begin blooming in July.

The *Northwest Native Plant Garden* was planted in 1964 by the Tacoma Garden Club. Its one-and-a-half acres display plants native to seven Pacific Northwest zones. This garden features a waterfall, pond, gazebo, totem, and basalt rock formation. The adjacent *Native Garden Meadow*, renovated by the Tacoma Garden Club in 2014, provides educational information on Pacific Northwest native plants.

In 1991, the Pierce County Iris Society established an *Iris Garden* that displays more than 100 bearded and 80 Pacific Coast hybrids. The *Fuchsia Garden* was planted by the Tahoma Fuchsia Society in 1994 and showcases more than 125 varieties of hardy fuchsias. Other display beds in the park include a perennial *Herb Garden,* the *Big Border,* and rose-covered arches. The Big Border and Rose Garden can be rented. Make inquires at (253) 305-1090.

Point Defiance Park covers more than 700 acres on a peninsula in Puget Sound. It is home to several state champion trees. Visitor can enjoy trails through old growth forest, beaches, the Point Defiance Zoo and Aquarium, and the Fort Nisqually Living History Museum. The park also has tennis courts, ball fields, and grass lawns. The *Visitor Center* in the park's historic lodge offers exhibits, maps, and a gift shop. See the Metro Park Tacoma website for more information.

<u>DIRECTIONS FROM SR 16</u>: *Take the Pearl St. Exit/SR 163 (south of the Tacoma Narrows Bridge). Follow Pearl St. north to Point Defiance Park. NOTE: The Tacoma Narrows Bridge has a toll in the southbound lanes.*

A beautiful Japanese maple and Torii Gate in the upper Japanese Garden

Point Defiance Park & Gardens
www.metroparkstacoma.org

Open daily from dawn to dusk, year-round
Dogs on-leash are welcome

- Approximately 10 acres of gardens in a 765-acre park
- No admission fee
- Picnicking permitted
- Restrooms available
- GIFT SHOP: Located in the park's Historic Lodge Visitor Center (open on weekends)
- STRUCTURES/FEATURES: Ponds, benches, gazebos, pavilion, rose-covered arbors and arches, waterfall, totem, wishing well, Japanese pagoda, teahouse, Torii Gate, Shinto Shrine, wooden signage identifying each garden area, grass lawns. Some structures can be rented.
- FEATURED PLANTS/COLLECTIONS: Irises, roses, dahlias, rhododendrons, azaleas, Northwest native plants, fuchsias, perennial herbs, Japanese maples, flowering cherry and crabapple trees, old-growth forest and rare trees
- ACTIVITIES: Pruning workshops, volunteer work parties, weekly rose deadheading work parties in summer, hiking and other recreational activities in Point Defiance Park. Garden Festival in fall. See *www.metroparkstacoma.org/garden-clubs-chip-in (under the "Gardens" tab on the Point Defiance Park page)* for information on volunteer opportunities in the park's gardens.
- TOURS: Self-guided tours only
- NEARBY ATTRACTIONS: Point Defiance Zoo and Aquarium, Fort Nisqually Living History Museum, hiking trails, Owen Beach (sunbathing, kayak rentals, refreshment stand), and a 5-mile drive around Point Defiance Park; Tacoma Nature Center and Preserve (1919 S. Tyler St., Tacoma), restaurants, shops, and museums along the Tacoma waterfront on Ruston Way; Tacoma's Chinese Reconciliation Park along Ruston Way; Brown's Point Lighthouse Park in Commencement Bay; Wapato Park (trail, off-leash dog park, and display gardens at 6500 S. Sheridan Ave.)
- NEARBY GARDENS: W.W. Seymour Conservatory, Lakewold Gardens, Rhododendron Species Botanical Garden, PowellsWood

The W.W. Seymour Conservatory is made of a steel frame and more than 3,000 panes of glass.

4 W. W. Seymour Conservatory
"A historical jewel in Tacoma"

Located in Tacoma's Wright Park

316 South G St.
Tacoma, WA 98405
(253) 591-5330
www.seymourconservatory.org
www.metroparkstacoma.org/conservatory

The W.W. Seymour Botanical Conservatory is a historic icon of Western Washington and one of the few remaining Victorian-style glass houses on the West Coast. The conservatory was built with a monetary gift of $10,000 given to the City of Tacoma by local resident and prosperous businessman, William W. Seymour, to be used for beautifying the city. The structure was opened in 1908, and in 1936 its name was changed to the W.W. Seymour Conservatory in honor of its donor. The conservatory celebrated its centennial in 2008 and is listed on the City of Tacoma, Washington State, and National Historic registers.

The 3,000-square-foot structure contains a 12-sided dome, two side wings, an entry wing, and more than 3,000 panes of glass. The building has undergone some changes, improvements, and necessary repairs over the years. In the 1940s, conservatory manager Clarence Deming replaced the concrete walkways with curved, brick paths that flow through the plant displays. He also added a koi pond, waterfall, Aztec-inspired statuary, and areas for changing floral displays.

The conservatory showcases more than 550 individual species of plants from all over the world and permanent collections of ferns, palms, figs, bromeliads, lilies, and over 200 orchids. It also displays collections of tender azaleas, cacti, tropical rhododendrons, clivias, cymbidiums (boat orchids), agapanthus, and exhibition chrysanthemums. Rare and unusual plants, including a giant Bird of Paradise that took 23 years to bloom, flourish in the building's warm environment. A selection of plants can be purchased in the conservatory's gift shop.

The conservatory is operated by Metro Parks Tacoma with funding support from the W.W. Seymour Conservatory Foundation. The foundation's mission is to "promote the connection between people and the natural world" *(the W.W. Seymour Conservatory Foundation website, 2014).* Many volunteers assist in fulfilling that mission.

Bromeliads create striking displays in the conservatory.

Conservatory visitors can enjoy a host of special events such as Children's Story Time, meditation sessions, garden parties, plant sales, art and floral exhibits, workshops, and Master Gardener clinics. Some events require registration and an additional fee. Self-guided tours are welcome during open hours. Guided group tours can be arranged by calling (253) 591-5330. The building can also be rented for weddings.

The conservatory is located in Wright Park, a 27-acre city park and arboretum that contains a collection of more than 630 native and exotic trees, and over a dozen state champion trees. The park is open daily, year-round and has public restrooms, a playground, pond, and lawn bowling court. Dogs are permitted in Wright Park, but only service animals are allowed in the conservatory. See the W.W. Seymour Conservatory website or the Tacoma Parks website for more information.

DIRECTIONS FROM I-5: Take the SR 16/ Bremerton Exit. Go north on SR 16, and take the Sprague St. Exit into Tacoma. Follow Sprague to 6th Ave. Turn right onto 6th Ave., then left onto G Street. Limited parking is available in front of the conservatory.

FROM SR 16: Take the 6th Ave. Exit. Go east. Continue past Wright Park, then turn left onto G Street.

The conservatory is filled with lush displays of tropical plants.

NOTE: There is a toll in the southbound lanes of the Tacoma Narrows Bridge on SR 16, north of Tacoma.

W.W. Seymour Conservatory

www.metroparkstacoma.org   www.seymourconservatory.org

Open Tuesday through Sunday, 10am-4:30pm, year-round
(open until 7pm on "free days")

- 3,000-square-foot Victorian-style glasshouse
- Admission fee on regular days. The third Thursday of every month is free admission.
- GIFT SHOP/PLANT SALES: Plants are sold in the conservatory's gift shop.
- STRUCTURES/FEATURES: More than 3,000 panes of glass, central glass dome, an entry wing and two side wings, koi pond, waterfall, benches, brick walkway, art displays, sculptures, outdoor gazebo
- FEATURED PLANTS/COLLECTIONS: Tropical rhododendrons, figs, tender azaleas, clivias, cymbidiums, agapanthus, bromeliads, lilies, over 200 orchids, exhibition chrysanthemums, cacti, palms, carnivorous plants, rare and unusual plants
- ACTIVITIES: Children's Story Hour, Grand Floral Display, member events, workshops, meditation sessions, garden parties, art and floral exhibits, Master Gardener clinics, volunteer opportunities. The building can be rented for weddings.
- TOURS: Self-guided tours are welcome. Guided school tours and private group tours can be arranged by calling (253) 591-5330.
- NEARBY ATTRACTIONS: Point Defiance Park (theme gardens, ponds, zoo, aquarium, living history museum, trails through old-growth forest, beach, marina); Tacoma restaurants, museums, and galleries; Tacoma Children's Museum (1501 Pacific Ave.); Tacoma Nature Center and Preserve (1919 S. Tyler St.); Tacoma's Chinese Reconciliation Park along Ruston Way; Browns Point Lighthouse Park; Wapato Park (trail, boating, off-leash dog park, and display gardens at 6500 S. Sheridan Ave., Tacoma)
- NEARBY GARDENS: The gardens at Point Defiance Park, Lakewold Gardens, Rhododendron Species Botanical Garden, PowellsWood

The Wagner House at Lakewold Gardens

5 Lakewold Gardens
"An inspirational garden experience"

Located in Lakewood's South Sound Lakes District

12317 Gravelly Lake Drive SW
Lakewood, WA 98499
(253) 584-4106
www.lakewoldgardens.org

The award-winning Lakewold Gardens originated as a family estate in 1908 with only five acres of land along Gravelly Lake. Now more than a century old, the estate and gardens cover 10 acres and are a state historic landmark. The estate was originally owned by the Alexander family. They built the existing Georgian-style house and installed the brick walk, perimeter fence, and other features. Acreage was added as the estate changed ownership, and in 1938, Eulalie Wagner and her husband, Corydon, purchased the estate that had been named "Lakewold" by its previous owners.

Mr. and Mrs. Wagner developed the estate into a world-class garden with plants and trees they collected from around the globe. They commissioned the help of landscape architect Thomas Church, who designed the garden's classical *European-style garden room* with Mt. Fuji cherry trees, boxwood display beds, a quatrefoil pool, and a rose-covered belvedere. Church also lined the estate's *Circle Drive* with rhododendrons (one of Mrs. Wagner's favorite plants) and installed a *Knot Garden* of culinary herbs near the house's veranda in memory of Mrs. Wagner's sister, Virginia Bloedel of the Bloedel Reserve.

The grounds at Lakewold display a mix of native and rare plants, flowering shrubs, flowers, and a variety of trees. The garden boasts collections of 10 state champion trees, over 30 varieties of Japanese maples, and more than 900 rhododendrons. The garden rooms are enhanced with beautiful architecture, statues made of French cast stone, and topiary. The *Hardy Fern Foundation's Display Garden,* located beside the Wagner House, showcases numerous ferns intermixed with interesting plants such as the mouse plant and bloodroot. The *Shade Garden* shows off pink dog-toothed violets and Himalayan blue poppies planted under a rare wolf tree that is hundreds of years old. In the *Woodland Garden,* a pond and stream create a peaceful setting among Japanese

Left: The Wagner House's solarium and wisteria-covered veranda. Right: One of the garden's many blue poppies.

A rare wolf tree is the focal point of the Shade Garden.

Mrs. Wagner often shared tea with her friends in Lakewold's rose-covered belvedere.

maples, a Chilean flame tree, and flowering shrubs. Alpine plants are featured in the *Rock Garden,* and a variety of other plants are displayed in the *Library Courtyard, Cutting Garden,* and the *Asian-inspired garden room.* Most of the rhododendrons peak in April, while other flowers continue to bloom through summer.

Mrs. Wagner donated her estate to the Friends of Lakewold, which formed in 1986. The garden opened to the public in 1989 and celebrated its 25th anniversary in May, 2014. The Friends of Lakewold's mission is "to preserve and enhance Lakewold Gardens as a historic estate garden of world-class distinction, offering each visitor an inspirational experience through growth and learning in a profoundly unique setting" *(the Lakewold Gardens website, 2014).* The pamphlet, *Garden Lover's Guide to the Pacific Northwest,* by Lakewold Gardens, and the coffee table book, *Lakewold: A Magnificent Northwest Garden,* edited by Ron Fields, provide more information about Lakewold and its history.

Garden improvements are made with Mrs. Wagner's vision in mind. In 2012, Lakewold Gardens added a program in which gardening groups adopt an area to plant and maintain. The Petal Pushers Garden Club was the first to participate, creating a beautiful bed of blue poppies, primroses, daffodils, and other perennials along the *Flag Pole Lawn,* near the *Hydrangea Bed*. Lakewold's *Garden Shop*, located in the original Carriage House, was redesigned in 2013. Plants are sold outside the Garden Shop when the garden is open.

The *Wagner House* is a significant feature of Lakewold with its spiral staircase, marble floor, crystal chandelier, wall murals, solarium, wisteria-covered veranda, and memorial library. The landscaping around the house is just as grand. The Wagner House is partially open during regular garden hours and can be viewed in its entirety during special events such as Mayfest and Beautiful Tables Showcase.

Lakewold offers a wide range of activities year-round, including Mayfest, Beautiful Tables Showcase, member events, workshops on gardening topics and crafts, and the Pinkerton Youth Program. Individuals can explore the garden on their own or register for a group tour. Garden space can be rented for weddings and private functions. See the Lakewold Gardens website for information on the garden and its programs.

DIRECTIONS FROM I-5: Take Exit 124 (Gravelly Lake Drive) and turn west onto Gravelly Lake Drive SW. At the Y, bear left and stay on Gravelly Lake Drive. The garden's entrance is just after the next traffic light (past Veteran's Drive), on the right.

Rhododendrons bordering Lakewold's lawns, paths, and Circle Drive shower the garden in color when they bloom.

Lakewold Gardens
www.lakewoldgardens.org

Open 10am-4pm (open until 8pm on Wednesdays in August).
Open Wednesday through Sunday, April through September;
Friday and Saturday, October through March

- 10 acres
- Admission fee
- Picnicking permitted
- Restrooms available
- GIFT SHOP: Located in the original 1918 Carriage House
- PLANT SALES: Plants are sold outside the gift shop.
- STRUCTURES/FEATURES: Wagner House, Garden Shop, French cast stone dog statues and other classic statuary, brick walkway, topiary, reflecting pool, pond, stream, waterfalls, stone steps, wisteria-covered veranda, knot garden, memorial benches, quatrefoil pool
- FEATURED PLANTS/COLLECTIONS: More than 900 rhododendrons, azaleas, bulbs, perennials, (hyacinth, peonies, alliums, hardy geraniums, Himalayan blue poppies, daffodils, primroses), woodland plants, flowering cherry and other ornamental trees, over 30 varieties of Japanese maples, ferns, a rare wolf tree, a Chinese Empress tree, a Chilean flame tree, exotic trees, 10 state champion trees
- ACTIVITIES: Seasonal and annual events such as Mayfest, Beautiful Tables Showcase, and Mother's Day Tea; classes for children and adults, Pinkerton Family Youth Program, volunteer work parties. Space can be rented for weddings.
- TOURS: Self-guided tours are welcome and do not require reservations. Guided public tours are offered, and private tours can be arranged for groups by calling (253) 584-4106.
- NEARBY ATTRACTIONS: Local parks (trails, playfields, swimming, golfing, playgrounds), Lakewood History Museum in the Old Colonial Center *(www.lakewoodhistorical.org)*, Fort Steilacoom Park *(www.cityoflakewood.us)*, Wild Waves Theme Park (Federal Way), Lewis Army Museum *(www.lewis-mcchord.army.mil)*, McChord Air Museum *(www.mcchordairmuseum.org)*
- NEARBY GARDENS: W. W. Seymour Conservatory, Point Defiance Park & Gardens, Rhododendron Species Botanical Garden, Powells-Wood, Chase Garden, Old Goat Farm

Hulda Klager's Victorian farmhouse was built by her father in the late 1800s. Photo courtesy of the Hulda Klager Lilac Society.

6 Hulda Klager Lilac Gardens
"An historic landmark"

Located in southwestern Washington, about 30 minutes north of Portland, Oregon

115 S. Pekin Rd.
Woodland, WA 98674
www.lilacgardens.com

The Hulda Klager Lilac Gardens is the legacy of a woman who was a horticulture pioneer. Hulda was fondly referred to as "the Lilac Lady" for the many varieties of lilacs she created on her farm of four-and-a-half acres in Woodland, Washington. Hulda immigrated to the U.S. from Germany with her parents as a child, and when she was a young girl, her family moved from Wisconsin to Woodland where they established a farm. Hulda later married Frank Klager, and they lived with their children in the Victorian farmhouse that has become a main attraction of the garden's annual Lilac Days event held in spring.

Hulda's interest in lilacs began when friends gave her a book written by hybridizer Luther Burbank while she was recovering from an illness. In 1905, Hulda started hybridizing lilacs herself, and by 1920 she had created so many lilac varieties that she started holding an open house every spring to sell them. Hulda was honored for her hybridizing work by many organizations and by the State of Washington, the City of Portland, and the Federation of Garden Clubs in Washington and Oregon. The garden she created at her home in Woodland now features lilacs in all sorts of colors, including white, pink, purple, blue, and bicolor, many of which are Hulda's varieties.

On more than one occasion, Hulda's farm came close to being lost forever. After a 1948 flood wiped out all of her plants except for some large trees, Hulda's friends replaced many of the lost lilacs by giving her ones that grew from starts they had previously bought from her. The Woodland Federated Garden Club later saved the farm from being developed and was instrumental in getting it designated as both a state and national historic site.

Hulda's father built the garden's *Victorian farmhouse* in the late 1800s. The house has been restored and is decorated with handmade quilts, antiques, artwork, and many furnishings that belonged to the Klager family. Many of the

A wide range of lilacs are propagated and sold at the garden during "Lilac Days." Right photo: 'White Madame Lemoine,' 'Purple Glory,' and 'Agincourt Beauty' lilacs. Right photo courtesy of the Hulda Klager Lilac Society.

The parlor and living room of Hulda's home. Left photo courtesy of the Hulda Klager Lilac Society.

display beds around the house were planted by Hulda and her parents, and the featured lilacs are displayed in a brick courtyard. A *Victorian Garden* of lilac hedges and flowering trees, a garden of *Pacific Northwest native plants,* a *Memorial Garden,* and a small arboretum also share the grounds.

The Hulda Klager Lilac Society purchased the farmhouse and gardens with the help of the Woodland community and the State of Washington. The society is a volunteer organization whose mission is "to preserve the lilac heritage developed by Hulda Klager and maintain the gardens for visitors to experience the tranquility of a pioneer Victorian farm and garden" *(the Hulda Klager Lilac Gardens website, 2014).*

The lilac gardens are maintained by the society's members and are open year-round. The society holds its annual *Lilac Days* event when the lilacs are blooming from mid-April to Mother's Day. During Lilac Days, the *farmhouse, potting shed,* and *Carriage House Gift Shop* are open, and volunteers are on hand to give information on the history of the garden. Lilacs can be purchased at that time. Proceeds from the event help support the garden. Visit the Hulda Klager Lilac Gardens website for details.

DIRECTIONS FROM I-5 SOUTHBOUND: Take Exit 21. Turn right onto Scott Ave., then left onto Pekin Rd. NORTHBOUND: Take Exit 21. Turn left onto Goerig St., bear right onto Davidson Ave., then turn left onto Pekin Rd. *Signs to the Lilac Gardens are posted near the I-5 exits and along the route through the town of Woodland.

Hulda Klager Lilac Gardens
www.lilacgardens.com

The grounds are open daily from 10am-4pm, year-round.
The farmhouse, gift shop, and other buildings are open during
Lilac Days from early April to Mother's Day.

- 4.5 acres
- Admission fee
- Picnicking permitted. Tables are on the lawn during Lilac Days.
- Restrooms are available during Lilac Days.
- GIFT SHOP: Located in the original Carriage Barn, open during Lilac Days.
- PLANT SALES: Lilacs are sold at the garden during Lilac Days.
- STRUCTURES/FEATURES: Potting shed, water tower, Carriage Barn, Victorian farmhouse (open during Lilac Days), brick walks, arbor, pergola; Adirondack chairs and other outdoor seating are provided during Lilac Days.
- FEATURED PLANTS/COLLECTIONS: Many varieties of lilacs, exotic trees, state champion umbrella tree, flowering shrubs, native plants, tulips
- ACTIVITIES: Lilac Days. Monthly meetings for Lilac Garden members are held in the Hulda Klager farmhouse.
- TOURS: Self-guided tours only; reservations not required. Garden clubs and other groups are welcome. Bus tour groups must schedule at least one week in advance by calling (360) 225-8996.
- NEARBY ATTRACTIONS: Woodland Historical Museum Society, downtown Woodland, Woodland Tulip Festival (April), Woodland Planters' Days (June). The garden is 30 minutes from Portland, OR.
- NEARBY GARDENS: Holland America Flower Gardens (tulip fields at 1066 S. Pekin Rd., *www.habg.net*); *In the Portland area*— the Japanese Garden *(www.japanesegarden.com)*, International Rose Test Garden *(www.portlandoregon.gov/parks)*, and Lan Su Chinese Garden *(www.lansugarden.org)*

The Chase House

7   Chase Garden
"A garden of timeless beauty"

Located on a bluff overlooking the Puyallup River Valley and Cascade foothills

16015 264th St. East
Orting, WA 98360
(360) 893-6739
www.chasegarden.org

Chase Garden was created from the imagination and passion of Emmott and Ione Chase. The garden consists of four-and-a-half acres on a bluff 200 feet above the Puyallup River, with an amazing view of the Cascade foothills. It is a splendid example of a naturalist garden inspired by Japanese-modernist design.

Emmott and Ione Chase were high school sweethearts and married in 1932. They both grew up in the Orting area, spending much of their childhood hiking the trails on Mt. Rainier. In the early part of their marriage, Emmott was a supervisor with Puget Sound Power and Light. He and Ione lived in company housing in Electron, Washington, where Emmott gained experience building stone walls and planting gardens.

When Emmott and Ione bought their 4.5 acres in 1942, blackberry bushes and old tree stumps covered the property. K. Walter Johnson built their house, and Emmott and Ione did most of the finishing work themselves. The landscaping around the house was designed by architect Rex Zumwalt. Emmott and Ione completed the terraces, reflecting pools, a covered lanai, a patio overlooking the lower lawn, and garden areas using mostly locally-found materials.

Ione designed most of the garden herself, and Emmott moved plants around the property until they were exactly where Ione wanted them. Ione filled her garden with color, planting trilliums, foxglove, fawn lilies, red columbine, and bear grass, and using ground covers generously. In the garden's *Woodland Path,* wild ginger, trilliums, vanilla leaf, and Hooker's fairybells thrive. The *Alpine Meadow* Ione designed is reminiscent of meadows on Mt. Rainier. Ione and Emmott also planted flowering dogwoods, a stand of noble firs, and ornamental shrubs, including pieris, enkianthus, many rhododendrons, and beds of heather. The *Summer Stroll Garden, Fern Walk,* and new plantings have been added in recent years. The Hardy Fern Foundation assisted with the Fern Walk installation.

In 1995, the Chases began working with the Garden

The Alpine Garden (left), rhododendrons (middle), and display beds by the house form a colorful canvas against a backdrop of evergreens.

The reflecting pool in the Entrance Garden

Conservancy to preserve their slice of paradise, and it was opened to the public on a limited basis. A horticultural manager and gardener were hired, and the Friends of Chase Garden was formed with a mission is to "continue the artistic vision of Emmott and Ione Chase and preserve their garden for public enjoyment and education" *(the Chase Garden website, 2014).* Plants and ground covers from the garden can be purchased on-site during open hours. There are future plans to open the house as a meeting place and expand the small nursery that features native plants and groundcovers from the garden.

The garden is open April through October. Spring Color and Fall Foliage weekends, Mother's Day and Father's Day openings, Holiday Tea and Tours, a Members Picnic, plant sales, and other events are held annually. Self-guided tours are welcome, and guided tours are offered the fourth Saturday of the month. Group tours can be scheduled by calling (360) 893-6739. See the Chase Garden website for more information.

DIRECTIONS FROM I-5: Take Exit 127 onto SR 512 East. Follow SR 512 to SR 161. Turn right onto SR 161 south (Meridian Ave.). Go about 10 miles, then turn left onto 264th St. East. Go another 3.7 miles and look for the sign at the garden entrance on the left. NOTE: To avoid heavy traffic on Meridian Ave., turn left onto 200th St. or 224th St. off Meridian Ave., and take the Orting Kapowsin Highway south from there to 264th St.

Chase Garden

www.chasegarden.org

Open Wednesday through Sunday, 10am-3pm
April through October

- 4.5 acres
- Admission fee
- Picnicking permitted
- Restrooms available
- PLANT SALES: Plants and ground covers from the garden are sold during garden hours and at the Friends of Chase Garden spring and fall plant sales.
- STRUCTURES/FEATURES: The Chase House, Japanese-inspired ponds and concrete foot bridges, dry stream bed, container plants, covered lanai and open terrace, large moss-covered rocks, river rock stepping stones, benches, panoramic view of the Cascade foothills and Mt. Rainier on a clear day. There are future plans to open the Chase House as a meeting place and expand the nursery.
- FEATURED PLANTS/COLLECTIONS: Rhododendrons, heather, enkianthus, pieris, woodland plants, alpine plants; native plants including foxglove, vanilla leaf, trilliums, red columbine, Hooker's fairybells, erythroniums (fawn lilies), and bear grass; ground covers, dogwoods, Noble firs, magnolias, Japanese maples
- ACTIVITIES: Holiday Tea and Tours, Spring Color and Fall Foliage weekends, Mother's Day and Father's Day openings, annual Members Picnic
- TOURS: Self-guided tours are welcome and do not require reservations. Guided tours are offered the fourth Saturday of every month from April through October. Private group tours can be arranged by calling (360) 893-6739.
- NEARBY ATTRACTIONS: Foothills Trail for pedestrians and bicycles (outside of Orting), Northwest Trek Wildlife Park, Mt. Rainier National Park, Mt. Rainier Scenic Railroad and Museum (in Elbe)
- NEARBY GARDENS: Lakewold Gardens, the Old Goat Farm

The Old Goat Farm's century-old Victorian farmhouse

8   Old Goat Farm
"A garden and nursery that step back in time"
(Angie Narus)

Located in a rural area above the Puyallup River Valley, north of Chase Garden

20021 Orting Kapowsin Hwy E.
Graham, WA 98338
(360) 893-1261
www.oldgoatfarm.com

This three-acre gem known as the Old Goat Farm is a wonderful mix of old and new. Visitors will find it hard not to fall in love with the charm of the 1903 *Victorian farmhouse* and its surrounding gardens, barn, nursery, and antique store that give a glimpse into the farm's past. Two acres of pasture provide space for the farm's goats and about 90 domestic birds, including peacocks.

The garden's borders have a balance of color and texture.

The old-fashioned nursery and store carry an assortment of treasures.

The farm's owners, Greg Graves and Gary Waller, previously lived on Capitol Hill in Seattle where they had an award-winning garden. Greg has a degree in Ornamental Horticulture and Landscape Design, was the head gardener at the Elisabeth C. Miller Botanical Garden in Shoreline for 13 years, is the board president for the Northwest Horticultural Society, and serves on the Great Plant Picks committee. Gary is AIFD certified, was a floral designer at Molbaks in Woodinville, and has won numerous awards for his floral and garden container designs. In the winter of 2004, Greg stumbled upon the farm outside of Orting while shopping for topiary with their friend, Linda. A few months later, Greg and Gary purchased the farm and soon began fixing it up.

When they bought the property, it was overgrown with blackberry bushes and weeds, and the existing flower beds were tired and in need of renovation. Greg and Gary removed the vines and weeds, and restored the soil. They planted maples, unique species of trees, new flower beds, and borders. Greg added ornamental trees and plants from places as far away as Tibet, giving the garden year-round interest.

Greg and Gary propagate about 75% of their plant material, putting the plants through a test period before adding them to the garden. Both Greg and Gary have their own signature on the garden's design. Gary planted the sunny borders, choosing daylilies and exotic flowers that create a balance of color and texture. He also designed numerous container plantings and installed several ponds and other water features in the garden.

Greg designs topiary. His work is integrated into the garden's design and displayed in the *Topiary Garden* he made in memory of their good friend, Linda. He also crafted the stone columns at the Topiary Garden's entrance, as well as the garden's fern tables and benches. In 2012, an ice storm wreaked havoc on the farm. After the storm, sixty truckloads of debris were hauled away, and Greg built a compost wall with what remained. The compost wall borders the nursery.

The Old Goat Farm's mission is "to offer well-grown garden plants in the garden's nursery that are also showcased in the garden" *(the Old Goat Farm website, 2014).* The garden, along with its old-fashioned nursery and garden store, is open to the public one weekend every month and at other times for guided tours and school field trips. Gary and Greg offer classes on a variety of gardening topics during the nursery season. They also host their popular Christmas Tea in December, when guests enjoy tea, desserts, and conversation with Gary and Greg in the farmhouse. For the event, Gary decorates every room with a different theme using ornaments and decorations he has been collecting for decades. Reservations are required for the Christmas Tea and other events. See the Old Goat Farm website for more information.

DIRECTIONS FROM I-5: Take Exit 161 onto SR 512. In about 8.5 miles, turn right onto SR 161/104th St. E. (Meridian Ave.) and continue for about 6 miles. Turn left onto 200th St. E. In about 2.4 miles, turn right onto Orting Kapowsin Hwy E. The garden is about 100 feet further on the left. (From Chase Garden, go about 4.2 miles north on Orting Kapowsin Hwy.

Visitors to the Old Goat Farm will encounter topiary, daylilies, and water features such as these in the garden.

Old Goat Farm

www.oldgoatfarm.com

Open on set dates one weekend per month from
April to October (check the website for dates and times).
Open other times for group tours, workshops, and special events.

- 3 acres
- No admission fee
- Picnicking not permitted for individuals on general visits. For a fee, groups with tour reservations can request a table be set up.
- Restrooms available
- GIFT SHOP: Garden decor (including handmade garden furniture), planters, books, and antique treasures are sold in the garden's store
- PLANT SALES: Plants are sold in the nursery during garden hours
- STRUCTURES/FEATURES: Victorian farmhouse (only open to the public for the Christmas Tea by reservation), barn, topiary, trellises, sculptures, compost wall, rock pillars, fountains, ponds, container plants, wooden Adirondack chairs and benches, animal shed, pasture, small farm animals including goats and domestic birds
- FEATURED PLANTS/COLLECTIONS: Spring ephemerals, daylilies, roses, rhododendrons, unique trees, topiary, container plants, native and exotic plants
- ACTIVITIES: Workshops on all aspects of gardening, lectures, Christmas Tea and other special events. Registration is required.
- TOURS: Self-guided tours are welcome on open dates and do not require reservations. Private tours for garden clubs and other groups, including school field trips, can be arranged by calling (360) 893-1261.
- NEARBY ATTRACTIONS: Foothills Trail for pedestrians and bicycles (outside of Orting), Northwest Trek Wildlife Park, Mt. Rainier National Park, Mt. Rainier Scenic Railroad and Museum (in Elbe)
- NEARBY GARDENS: Chase Garden, Lakewold Gardens

The pond at PowellsWood is a calm, refreshing spot to sit and enjoy the garden.

9 PowellsWood
"A Northwest pleasure garden"

Located in a residential area of Federal Way

430 S. Dash Point Rd.
Federal Way, WA 98003
www.powellswood.org

Nestled in an urban, residential area of Federal Way is a three-acre garden named PowellsWood that was truly designed to "restore the soul." This peaceful garden is located on a three-acre portion of a 40-acre greenbelt, owned by Federal Way residents, Monte and Diane Powell, in partnership with the PowellsWood Garden Foundation.

After years of land and soil restoration, the Powells created a beautiful garden at the edge of a native woodland, buffered by a screen of tall hedges on one side and a ravine on the other. The site's ravine was formerly a Cold Creek watershed stream that dried up when the water level of a nearby aquifer was lowered. The three acres were put up for sale, and in 1993, Monte and Diane purchased the property with the intent to preserve it for public use.

The Powells spent two years removing rubble, asphalt, old cars, tires, and other debris from the section of the property that would become the cultivated garden, and they amended the soil to support plant life. Landscape architect Ned Gulbran was the garden's first designer. His plan included rows of hedges, perennial beds, and garden rooms installed in stages. Ned continues to consult with the Powells on garden projects.

PowellsWood underwent a renovation in 2013 with the design services of Rick Serazin. The garden now contains more than 1,000 varieties of plants, including flowers such as roses, fuchsias, hellebores, Asian lilies, and anemones, as well as unique conifers, native plants, 15 varieties of hydrangeas, and 25 varieties of rhododendrons. The garden also showcases many plants that have a tropical appearance such as hardy *Schefflera*, windmill palms, and rosy crabapple kiwi in tropical-inspired plantings.

The *Entry Garden* welcomes visitors with stone birdbaths set among palms and other plants in a central display bed. From there, a rustic arbor opens to the rest of the garden. One branch of the path passes by the *Garden House* and its brick patio where tables and umbrellas are set up for

Left to right: One of several stone birdbaths in the Entry Garden, the brick walk leading to the Garden House, and a cluster of banana plants.

The variety of display beds at PowellsWood show a wide spectrum of color and texture. The design creates a unifying flow with the repetition of certain plants throughout the garden.

visitors. The house's *Garden Room* is used as a meeting place and information center, and can be rented for private events.

Another branch of the path continues along the *Rhododendron and Fern Border,* down a slope and stairs, along a *Perennial Border,* to the garden's recirculating pond. As water from seasonal runoff flows into the pond, it is pumped back uphill, providing an ecological benefit by allowing sediment to settle out of the water before reaching Puget Sound. The path continues past the *Shade Garden* where clematis and climbing roses cover a long arbor, to an overlook made mostly with boards from an old pier in the *Woodland Garden.* The Shade Garden and Woodland Garden demonstrate how homeowners can use natural features to create beautiful landscapes. Continuing from the Woodland Garden, the path soon merges with a lawn bordered by cherry trees and flowers in the *Spring Garden*, before circling back to the Garden House. As seen throughout PowellsWood, the garden staff use sustainable gardening methods and recycled materials to build new garden structures whenever possible.

Monte's trips to England, where he studied European horticulture and worked as an intern at the Harlow Carr Garden, influenced PowellsWood's design. Monte and Diane believe green spaces such as this can improve the quality of life for people living in urban areas, and they have worked with the Garden Conservancy to take PowellsWood into the future.

Monte and Diane support the Friends of the Children's Eternal Rainforest, a "non-profit organization dedicated to the protection, support, and expansion of the Children's Eternal Rainforest in Monte Verde, Costa Rica" *(www.friends oftheeternalrainforest.org).* They also support nature education for children and youth, and founded a program that provides South Seattle College Landscape Horticulture students internship opportunities at the Harlow Carr Garden.

PowellsWood is open to the public from April through October. Visitors are welcome to explore the garden on their own during open hours. Guided tours can be scheduled for school groups, garden clubs, and other groups by calling (253) 529-1620. PowellsWood hosts annual events such as a Mother's Day Tea, an Earth Day celebration, and a well-attended Storytelling Festival. The Storytelling Festival is a fun, two-day event held every July, co-sponsored by the Seattle Storytellers' Guild. Visit the PowellsWood website for more information on these and other garden events offered at the garden.

DIRECTIONS FROM I-5: *Take Exit 147 and go west on South 272nd St. Turn left onto Pacific Hwy S., then right onto SR 509/South Dash Point Rd. Go about 1 mile to the entrance on the right.*

A soft blanket of snow covers the Entry Garden and its arbor. Photo courtesy of PowellsWood.

PowellsWood

www.powellswood.org

Open Tuesday through Saturday, 10am-3pm
April through October

- 3 acres
- Admission fee
- Picnicking permitted
- Restrooms available
- STRUCTURES/FEATURES: Conservatory-style Garden Room (in the Garden House), pond, hedges, ravine overlook, benches, vine-covered arbors, stone birdbaths, benches, sculptures, brick walk and patio with tables and umbrellas, steps, grass lawn
- FEATURED PLANTS/COLLECTIONS: Tropical-inspired plantings; banana plants, hardy Schefflera, windmill palms, rosy crabapple kiwi; rhododendrons, hydrangeas, fuchsias, Asian lilies, anemones, water-loving plants, unique conifers, magnolias and other flowering trees, native woodland
- ACTIVITIES: Annual Mother's Day Tea, annual Storytelling Festival, Garden Conservancy Open Days, Earth Day celebration, gardening-related classes for children and adults, school field trips
- TOURS: Self-guided tours are welcome and do not require reservations. Guided tours for individuals and groups can be arranged through the website.
- NEARBY ATTRACTIONS: Dash Point State Park, Wild Waves Theme Park (on Enchantment Parkway, *www.wildwaves.com*); Trampoline Nation (on Enchantment Parkway, *www.trampolinenation.com*)
- NEARBY GARDENS: Rhododendron Species Botanical Garden, the Pacific Rim Bonsai Collection (adjacent to the Rhododendron Species Botanical Garden), Soos Creek Botanical Garden, W. W. Seymour Conservatory, Point Defiance Park and Gardens

Tropical rhododendrons and unusual plants thrive in the garden's Rutherford Conservatory.

10 Rhododendron Species Botanical Garden

"Where the wild things grow"

Located in Federal Way, just a few minutes off I-5

2525 S. 336th St.
Federal Way, WA 98003
(253) 838-4646
www.rhodygarden.org

The Rhododendron Species Botanical Garden is an amazing place to view more than 700 *Rhododendron* species. It is one of the first public gardens to be devoted to the preservation and cultivation of a single genus, and has one of the best collections of documented wild plant material on the West Coast. The garden is both a research facility and public garden covering 22 acres, operated by a staff under the direction of a Board of Directors. Many volunteers help maintain the garden.

The beginnings of the Rhododendron Species Botanical Garden can be traced back to Dr. Milton Walker, the first president of the Rhododendron Species Foundation. The foundation was started in response to a concern for rhododendron habitat being destroyed in many parts of the world. Dr. Walker had begun collecting cuttings of rhododendrons from public and private gardens in England. As his collection grew, it eventually became too large to be housed in the private gardens of foundation board members, and in 1975, the board arranged to lease land for free on Weyerhaeuser Corporation property in Federal Way as a permanent site for the collection. The foundation celebrated its 50th anniversary in 2014, continuing its mission to "the conservation, research, acquisition, evaluation, cultivation, public display, and distribution of *Rhododendron* species" *(the Rhododendron Species Botanical Garden website, 2013).*

The Rhododendron Species Botanical Garden has several themed areas, including the *Alpine Rock Garden, Pond Garden, Magnolia Grove, Japanese Azalea Garden, giant Himalayan lilies,* a meadow of more than 500 *Himalayan*

The Pond Garden

The Victorian Stumpery, established in 2009 by the Hardy Fern Foundation, is an interesting arrangement of root balls and stumps that provide habitat for more than 100 species of ferns.

(Tibetan) blue poppies, and a *big leaf rhododendron forest.* The garden exhibits *Rhododendron* species from around the world, as well as collections of Liliaceae, primula, ferns, woodland wildflowers, hardy Ericaceae (plants in the heath family), and Japanese maples. Many of the garden's specimens come from plant-hunting expeditions led by Executive Director, Steve Hootman.

The garden also has an amazing collection of tree species such as magnolias, mountain ashes, Asian conifers, and numerous Styracaceae (a small family of flowering shrubs and trees). Look carefully for rare Asian vines growing on some of the trees. The garden's *Victorian Stumpery* (pictured above) is an intriguing display of more than 100 species of ferns in a habitat of stumps and root balls. The stumpery is the main study garden of the Hardy Fern Foundation and is the largest public stumpery in the world. See *www.hardy ferns.org* for more information.

The garden's *Rutherford Conservatory* opened in 2010. The 5,000-square-foot glass conservatory displays a collection of tropical rhododendrons called vireyas, their relatives, other tropical plants, and unusual flowers. The conservatory provides a natural-looking environment with a stream, waterfall, and rock structures, where plants can be viewed by visitors all year. Other garden areas, accessible paths, and more nursery space have been added to the garden in recent years.

Plants propagated at the garden are sold in the on-site nursery. The plant sale area, located between the gift shop and conservatory, is open during garden hours and special plant sales. The selection of plants available for purchase changes throughout the year.

The Rhododendron Species Botanical Garden holds a variety of annual events and activities such as Blue Poppy Day in May, a Fall Foliage Festival in October, a large plant sale, and classes on gardening topics. Visitors can tour the garden on their own, and guided tours can be arranged by calling (253) 838-4646. Garden space and the *Rutherford Conservatory* can be rented for weddings and private functions. More information is available on the Rhododendron Species Botanical Garden website.

DIRECTIONS FROM I-5: Take Exit 142 to SR 18 East, or Exit 143 to 320th St. Get onto Weyerhaeuser Way. Go north around the traffic circle, and follow the signs to the garden. *FROM SR 18*: Take the Weyerhaeuser Way Exit, go north on Weyerhaeuser Way around the traffic circle, and follow the signs to the garden.

FROM POWELLSWOOD: Go left on Dash Point Rd. Turn right onto SR 99/ Pacific Hwy, then left onto S. 336th. Go under the I-5 overpass, bear right onto Weyerhaeuser Way, and follow the signs to the garden.

Rhododendron Species Botanical Garden

www.rhodygarden.org

The garden, conservatory, and nursery are open
Tuesday through Sunday, 10am-4pm, year-round
(closed on some holidays).
The Rutherford Conservatory is included with general admission

- 22 acres
- Picnicking permitted on the Rutherford Conservatory terrace
- Restrooms available
- GIFT SHOP: Garden Shop located at the garden entrance
- PLANT SALES: Plants are sold at the garden's Plant Sale Pavilion during garden hours and during special plant sales
- STRUCTURES/FEATURES: Rutherford Conservatory, Plant Sale Pavilion and nursery, sculptures, pond, gazebo, benches
- FEATURED PLANTS/COLLECTIONS: Over 700 *Rhododendron* species, Lilaceae, Styracaceae, magnolias, Asian conifers, alpine plants, water-loving plants, giant Himalayan lilies, hundreds of Himalayan blue poppies, azaleas, primroses, woodland wildflowers, hardy Ericaceae, Japanese maples tropical plants, rare trees from around the world
- ACTIVITIES: Annual Blue Poppy Day, annual Fall Foliage Festival, member events, classes, workshops, lectures, volunteer opportunities
- TOURS: Garden maps can be downloaded from the garden's website for self-guided tours. Self-guided tours do not require reservations. Guided tours can be arranged by calling (253) 838-4646.
- NEARBY ATTRACTIONS: Pacific Rim Bonsai Collection, downtown Tacoma (museums, galleries, restaurants), Dash Point State Park in Federal Way, Wild Waves Theme Park (on Enchantment Parkway, *www.wildwaves.com*), Trampoline Nation (on Enchantment Parkway, *www.trampolinenation.com*), Northwest Trek Wildlife Park, Mt. Rainier National Park
- NEARBY GARDENS: PowellsWood, Soos Creek Botanical Garden, W.W. Seymour Conservatory, Lakewold Gardens, Old Goat Farm, Chase Garden

The Pond Garden and the opposing long borders lay almost perpendicular to each other, creating a balanced view of the garden landscape.

11   Soos Creek Botanical Garden & Heritage Center

"A unique pairing of plants and history"
(Angie Narus)

Located off SR 18, near Kent

29308 132nd Ave. SE
Auburn, WA 98092
(253) 639-0949
www.sooscreekbotanicalgarden.org

The 23-acre Soos Creek Botanical Garden and Heritage Center is a testament to what can be learned by observation, a couple of botany classes, and a love of plants. The garden began with five rural acres Maurice Skagen's parents had given him. The property was part of a 200-acre plat on the Soos Creek Plateau that was originally owned by the Skagen family's Norwegian ancestors.

Maurice recalls that there was a time when the woods on the property were so dense a horse could not be ridden through them. He had intended to preserve the property as open space for the community, but with diligence, hard work, and his knowledge of plants, Maurice instead transformed the acreage into a series of beautiful garden rooms and stroll gardens dedicated to the memory of his parents, relatives, and friends.

Maurice started developing his garden during graduate school, using conifers, azaleas, rhododendrons, and other plants he collected for his master's thesis. Memories of his aunt's vividly-colored flower beds and his frequent trips to England and Japan in the 1980s inspired his design. Many of the plants in his garden grew from seeds he brought back from those trips.

This is truly a garden of many colors. One path winds its way through collections of camellias, hydrangeas, magnolias, roses, rhododendrons, kalmias, ericas, pieris, maples, and numerous exotic trees and shrubs. The *Fenzl Garden Room,* adjacent to the house, is filled with flowers such as hardy fuchsia, climbing roses, and unusual shrubs and trees. Maurice's Aunt Nettie's flower garden was the inspiration for the *Heritage Flower Garden* which features irises, peonies, and other spring flowers. *Aucuba japonica* (spotted laurel), rhododendrons, hydrangeas, and azaleas are but a handful of

The garden has a balance of color and texture, from white viburnums and rhododendrons to purple peonies.

the specimens that line the brick walk around the house.

The garden's centerpiece is the *Schaefer Pond Garden,* created on what used to be a bog area. The quiet pond, floating lily pads, cattails, and other plants hug the pond's banks like a scene from a storybook. Possibly the most prominent features of the garden are the two opposing, 500-foot-long borders that run down both sides of the sloped lawn below the pond. A variety of unique trees, flowers, and shrubs create a kaleidoscope of color and texture in the borders.

Paths lead through other display areas, including the *Cedar Grove, Ravine Garden, Rain Garden, Alder Grove,* and *Vegetable Demonstration Garden,* and past an *Aviary* of tropical birds (adjacent to the house). Maurice recently installed two *native plant gardens* as well—one for shade and one for sun—on either side of the Soos Creek tributary that runs through the property. Many of the garden's other improvements can be credited to local Boy Scouts working toward earning their Eagle Scout designation.

The *Soos Creek Heritage Center* is a unique feature Maurice built in an effort to preserve the rural history of the area and the Skagen family heritage. The center's historical photos, maps, articles, old tools, and furnishings depict farm life of settlers on the Soos Creek plateau. It is open to the public during garden hours for personal research and cultural interest.

Maurice and his partner in the garden, James Daly, live on the property. Their house was built in a style that showcases the timber produced at local sawmills. Maurice and James started the Garden Foundation in 2009 and opened their garden to the public in 2011. The Garden Foundation's mission is "to provide a diversity of gardens for the public to enjoy...while providing education and conservation of horticulture, the environment, and history" *(the Soos Creek Botanical Garden website, 2014)*. More than 30 volunteers assist Maurice and James with planning, maintenance, and administrative tasks. A mixture of ideas, knowledge, and skills has been brought to the garden as more people have become involved.

The Soos Creek Botanical Garden holds public events and workshops on various gardening topics. Self-guided tours are welcome, and guided tours can be arranged for groups by calling (253) 639-0949. A donation is suggested for admission. See the Soos Creek Botanical Garden website for more information.

<u>DIRECTIONS FROM I-5</u>: *Take the Auburn-North Bend Exit (SR 18). Go east on SR 18. Take the SE 304th Exit off SR 18. Turn right onto SE 304th St., then right onto 132nd Ave. SE. In about one mile, watch for the garden entrance on the right.*

A mixture of plants in the long borders forms a kaleidoscope of color and texture.

Soos Creek Botanical Garden

www.sooscreekbotanicalgarden.org

Open Wednesday through Saturday, 10am-3pm
mid-March to mid-November

- 23 acres
- Suggested donation for admission
- Picnicking not permitted
- Restrooms available
- PLANT SALES: Annual spring and fall plant sale
- STRUCTURES/FEATURES: Private residence, Heritage Center, barns, tropical bird aviary, greenhouse, pond, a walking bridge built on a fallen Douglas Fir, benches, pergola, arbor, trellises, sculptures and other embellishments
- FEATURED PLANTS/COLLECTIONS: Collections of camellias, heath, hydrangeas, magnolias, maples, pieris, rhododendrons, roses, and kalmias; numerous azaleas, hellebores, winter-blooming jasmine, peonies, Japanese maples, unique trees, large-leaf plants such as banana and gunnera
- ACTIVITIES: Special events, workshops on various gardening topics, volunteer opportunities
- TOURS: Self-guided tours are welcome and do not require reservations. Guided group tours can be arranged by contacting *tours@ sooscreekbotanicalgarden.org* two weeks in advance.
- NEARBY ATTRACTIONS: Lake Meridian Park, Northwest Trek Wildlife Park, Mt. Rainier National Park, Kent
- NEARBY GARDENS: Rhododendron Species Botanical Garden, PowellsWood, Lake Wilderness Arboretum

The Lake Wilderness Arboretum's plant collections are displayed in a peaceful, woodland setting.

12 Lake Wilderness Arboretum

"42 acres of gardens and forest that are sure to delight and inspire every visitor"

Adjacent to Lake Wilderness Park in Maple Valley

22520 SE 248th Ave.
Maple Valley, WA 98038
(425) 413-2572
www.lakewildernessarboretum.org

The Lake Wilderness Arboretum consists of 42 acres of second-growth forest reserve, cultivated gardens, and hiking trails. In 1965, then-recent immigrant George Tersiisky introduced the idea for an arboretum in South King County. The vision was brought to reality by the development of the South King County Arboretum Foundation, which later became the Lake Wilderness Arboretum Foundation. In 1967, the foundation was given approval to establish an arboretum at the former Gaffney Resort by Lake Wilderness. The

Allium ursinum (wild garlic)

resort's old corral was converted into a nursery where plant sales have been held every year since the arboretum's inception.

In 1970, an architect designed the grounds, and a master plan was developed. The plan has guided the Arboretum Foundation's mission "to preserve and develop beautiful green spaces that showcase Northwest ecosystems for present and future generations" *(the Lake Wilderness Arboretum website, 2013).*

These peaceful gardens make up about five acres at the edge of the arboretum's forested area. A gazebo and benches provide places to relax, while trellises and a water feature add artistic elements to the gardens. The garden paths are lined with kalmias, irises, hellebores, trilliums, large patches of hardy cyclamen, and other flowers. The *Tribal Life Trail* highlights plants used by Northwest Native Americans.

The arboretum's plant collections include hydrangeas, daylilies, rhododendrons, and western azaleas. The collections and other plants are displayed as groupings in the *Alpine Garden, Japanese Maple Garden, Perennial Garden, Smith-Mossman Western Azalea Garden, Volunteer Garden, Rhododendron Garden,* and *Legacy Garden.* The *Rhododendron Garden* showcases the collections donated by George Steuber in memory of his wife, Lillie. The *Legacy Garden* similarly preserves the collections of Loie Benedict and Marjorie Baird. The arboretum holds the title for having the

Western azalea

Colorful specimens in the arboretum's rhododendron collection

largest selection of western azaleas in the world and one of the largest collections of hardy fuchsias in the Pacific Northwest.

The Lake Wilderness Arboretum is one of the few remaining public gardens in South King County. It is maintained by a partnership between the Lake Wilderness Arboretum Foundation, community volunteers, and the City of Maple Valley. Volunteer work parties are held on special days such as Make a Difference Day and the United Way Day of Caring. Festivals, educational programs, outdoor theater, and other events are held at the arboretum throughout the year, and the foundation has huge, annual spring and fall plant sales. The arboretum and gardens are open for public use year-round, and free public tours are offered one Saturday each month from April to October. Tours can be arranged for groups at other times by calling (253) 293-5103. For more information, visit the Lake Wilderness Arboretum website.

DIRECTIONS FROM I-5 OR SR 18: Take the exit to the Maple Valley Hwy 169. Turn right onto 232 St., then right onto Maple Valley Hwy 169. Turn right onto Witte Rd., and follow Witte Rd. until you get to the roundabout. Take the third exit out of the roundabout onto SE 248th St. The arboretum is straight ahead on the left, before the Lake Wilderness Lodge. Follow the signs to the arboretum's main parking area, before the lodge.

Lake Wilderness Arboretum
www.lakewildernessarboretum.org

Open daily from dawn to dusk, year-round
Dogs on-leash are welcome

- 42 acres of forest reserve, cultivated gardens, and hiking trails
- No admission fee
- Picnicking permitted
- Restrooms available in the adjacent Lake Wilderness Park
- PLANT SALES: Annual spring and fall plant sale organized by the Lake Wilderness Arboretum Foundation
- STRUCTURES/FEATURES: Nursery, gazebo, trellises, arbors, pond, benches, interpretive signs along the Tribal Life Trail, hiking on the arboretum's Green-to-Cedar Trail
- FEATURED PLANTS/COLLECTIONS: Japanese maples; collections of western azaleas, hardy fuchsias, hydrangeas, daylilies, and rhododendrons; kalmias, vine maples, hellebores, trilliums, ferns, hardy cyclamen, flowering dogwoods, alpine plants
- ACTIVITIES: Annual events including the Hellebore Tea fundraiser, Western Azalea Celebration, holiday light display, outdoor theater productions, school and youth programs, volunteer work parties
- TOURS: Self-guided tours are welcome. Public tours are offered one Saturday per month from April to October. Private tours can be arranged for groups by calling (253) 293-5103.
- NEARBY ATTRACTIONS: Lake Wilderness Park (picnic areas, tennis courts, open grass areas, lake, pool, boating), historic Lake Wilderness Lodge, Mt. Rainier National Park
- NEARBY GARDENS: Soos Creek Botanical Garden

The central pond in Elda Behm's Paradise Garden is surrounded by flowering shrubs, ornamental grasses, and trees.

13   Highline SeaTac Botanical Garden
"Preserving our garden heritage—Growing our future"

Located at the North SeaTac Community Center, one mile north of the Seattle-Tacoma International Airport

13735 24th Ave. W.
SeaTac, WA 98168
(206) 391-4003
www.highlinegarden.org

The Highline SeaTac Botanical Garden is thought to be the only public garden in the U.S. devoted to rescuing gardens slated for demolition due to city growth and airport expansion. The garden is on an 11.5-acre site in North SeaTac Park, donated by the City of SeaTac at the request of enthusiastic volunteers wanting an urban oasis.

Garden expert Elda Behm (pronounced "beam") and her husband spent nearly 35 years turning their suburban lot near the Seattle-Tacoma International Airport into an

Planted containers (left) and the garden's entrance gate (above) add decorative elements and visual balance to the garden.

award-winning cottage garden. In the late 1990s, the Port of Tacoma approached Elda about purchasing her property to make room for a third runway. To save her garden, the Highline Botanical Garden Foundation, the City of Tacoma, and the Port of Seattle, joined with Elda to move her plants to North SeaTac Park. Together, they created a replica of Elda's *Paradise Garden* with a pond, seasonal stream, waterfalls, pergola, a variety of uncommon plants, a collection of rhododendrons, and a shade garden.

The *Seiki Japanese Garden* was the second garden to be saved by the foundation. The pond-and-mountain-style garden was initially built in the early 1960s at the Seiki family nursery as a memorial to their son who was killed in WWII while serving in the U.S. Army. When the nursery was in the path of another proposed runway, a team made up of the City of SeaTac, the State of Washington, a local contractor, the Seiki family, and volunteers relocated the memorial garden to North SeaTac Park using photos and blueprints. The Japanese Garden is small but nevertheless remarkable with a path that crosses a central pond by way of foot bridges and rocks, and weaves between boulders, stone lanterns, sculptures, pines, azaleas, and other plants. Members of the Seiki family continue to help maintain the garden alongside other volunteers.

Being only one mile from the airport, this garden was designed to be an urban retreat. Three and a half acres have been developed so far. Local gardening groups, including the Puget Sound Daylily Club, King County Iris Society, Puget Sound Fuchsia Club, and the Seattle Rose Society, plant and tend the beds of daylilies, fuchsias, and roses. The *Rose Garden* surrounds a formal event lawn. The rose-covered arches at the event lawn's entrance fill with color when the roses bloom. A *Heritage Garden* is being planned to honor previous homes that were demolished at the site when the airport was built. A visitor center, Natural Yard Care Garden, and other features will also be added as developed by the Design Committee.

The Highline Botanical Garden Foundation operates the garden in partnership with the SeaTac Parks Department. The foundation's mission is "to manage and develop a community-owned garden based on a plant collection that demonstrates the best horticulture and environmental practices, and that creates beauty for public enjoyment" *(the Highline SeaTac Botanical Garden website, 2014).* Summer concerts, an Ice Cream Social with guest speakers and vendors, plant sales, and workshops are help at the garden each year. Guided tours can be arranged for groups by calling (206) 391-4003. Visit the Highline SeaTac Botanical Garden website for more information.

DIRECTIONS FROM SR 518 WESTBOUND (off I-5): Take the exit for 154th St. off of SR 518. At the stop sign, turn left onto 154th St., then right onto 24th Ave. Go north one mile, then turn left at the entrance to the North SeaTac Community Center at 136th St.

The Seiki Japanese Garden

Highline SeaTac Botanical Garden

www.highlinegarden.org

Open daily from dawn to dusk, year-round
Dogs on-leash are welcome

- 3.5 acres developed (on an 11.5-acre site)
- No admission fee
- Picnicking not permitted
- Portable restroom available
- PLANT SALES: Annual spring and fall plant sale
- STRUCTURES/FEATURES: Metal entrance gate, metal arbors, trellises, ponds, seasonal stream, waterfalls, boulders, stone lanterns, foot bridges, container plants, benches, sculptures, pergola, interpretive signs; a formal event lawn bordered by columns, arbors, and rose beds. The event lawn can be reserved for weddings.
- FEATURED PLANTS/COLLECTIONS: *Rhododendron* collection, companion woodland plants, shade-loving plants, ornamental grasses, Japanese maples, irises, fuchsias, daylilies, roses, azaleas, pines, deciduous trees
- ACTIVITIES: Summer musical performances, Ice Cream social, classes and workshops on gardening topics, volunteer work parties
- TOURS: Self-guided tours are welcome. Public tours are sometimes offered on volunteer work party days. Guided tours can be arranged for groups by calling (206) 391-4003.
- NEARBY ATTRACTIONS: Boeing Field and the Museum of Flight, nearby skate park and remote-control car track, Seahurst Park along the Burien waterfront (1600 SE Seahurst Park Rd.)
- NEARBY GARDENS: SeaTac Senior Center's sensory garden (across the parking lot from the botanical garden), the Japanese Garden at SeaTac City Hall (4800 S. 188th St.), Kubota Garden, South Seattle College Arboretum, Seattle Chinese Garden

The impressive, bronze sliding gate at the Kubota Garden entrance was designed by artist Gerard Tsutakawa.

14 Kubota Garden
"Seattle's hidden treasure"

Located in the Rainier Beach neighborhood of South Seattle, near Tukwila

9817 55th Ave. S.
Seattle, WA 98178
(206) 684-4584
www.kubotagarden.org   www.seattle.gov/parks

The Kubota Garden is a stunning, American-Japanese garden that began on five acres of logged swampland and now consists of 20 acres plus a bordering 27-acre natural area. The garden was designed by Fujitaro Kubota, who came to the U.S. from Japan as a young man. Mr. Kubota was a self-taught gardener and established the Kubota Gardening Company, designing gardens with Japanese influences throughout the Puget Sound area, including the Japanese Garden at

Four of the garden's amazing bridges (left to right): Moon Bridge, a stone bridge in the Japanese Garden, Heart Bridge, and a stone plank bridge spanning Mapes Creek.

the Bloedel Reserve, the Rainier Club in downtown Seattle, and many of the gardens on the campus of Seattle University.

In 1927, Mr. Kubota purchased the Rainier Beach property as the site for his landscaping business. Over the next 25 years, he transformed it into a garden where he displayed unique trees, ornamental shrubs, and flowers in natural settings. Mr. Kubota and his wife lived on the property and frequently hosted social and cultural activities for the local Japanese community in the display garden that Mr. Kubota was creating. His son, Tom, continued his legacy.

The garden's *Entry Plaza* near the parking lot welcomes visitors with rhododendrons, azaleas, flowers, trees, and a stone garden. The Entry Plaza offers a snapshot of what lies beyond the ornate, sliding entrance gate designed by artist Gerard Tsutakawa. There is much to explore in this garden, and "when you walk through the gate, you enter another world," *(Joe Toynbee, Tour Guide for the Kubota Garden Foundation).* The *Japanese Garden, Mountainside Trail, Stroll Garden, Woodland Trail,* and *Rock Garden* are mixed with nooks, grottos, spring-fed ponds, waterfalls, and Japanese-style foot bridges. The picturesque bridges (shown above) have names such as the *Heart Bridge,* set in the heart of the garden, and the *Moon Bridge,* designed to be hard to walk over because of its steep arch. Other stone bridges span Mapes Creek, which flows through the garden.

Mr. Kubota built the garden's somewhat steep *Mountainside Trail* to celebrate the 1962 Seattle World's Fair. The trail climbs the hillside to a lookout that gives a birds-eye view of the garden 64 feet below. Tom Kubota designed the *Stroll Garden* with colorful beds of flowers, shrubs, and a pond surrounding a grass lawn (pictured below). The new *Terrace Overlook,* constructed in 2014, is an open-air structure that provides a covered place for visitors to enjoy views of the garden. A *Visitor Center* is also being planned.

The Kubota Garden showcases numerous weeping trees, including a 32-foot-long weeping blue Atlas cedar, several weeping Norway spruce, and weeping deodar cedars. There are also groupings of heather, rhododendrons, azaleas, Japanese maples, giant camellias, deciduous trees, and a grove of threadleaf cypress. Three of the oldest trees in the garden are a Japanese pine, an umbrella pine, and a grand fir that is hundreds of years old.

In 1987, the City of Seattle acquired the garden from the Kubota family. The garden is now maintained by the Department of Parks and Recreation, a small staff including a head gardener, and many volunteers. The Kubota Garden Foundation was formed to "support, enhance, and perpetuate

The Tom Kubota Stroll Garden bursts with color in spring and summer.

Large boulders like these in the Rock Garden are a key feature of the Kubota Garden.

the Kubota Garden within the spirit of Fujitaro Kubota and his son, Tom Kubota" *(the Kubota Garden website, 2014).* The foundation offers tours and supports the garden through plant sales and special events. The Kubota Garden is open to the public seven days a week, year-round. Free, public tours are offered the fourth Saturday of every month, and tours can be arranged for groups by calling (206) 725-5060. Visit the Kubota Garden website for more information and for a more detailed history of the garden's development. To reserve garden space for weddings and other private functions, contact the Department of Parks and Recreation at (206) 684-4080.

DIRECTIONS FROM I-5 SOUTHBOUND: *Take the Pacific Hwy/East Marginal Way Exit. Cross over I-5, then go straight onto Ryan Way and continue up the hill. *At the flashing light at the top of the hill, turn left onto 51st St. Turn right onto Roxbury at the Y, then make an immediate right onto Renton Ave. Go a short distance up the hill, turn right onto 55th Ave., then make a right into the garden's parking area.*

FROM I-5 NORTHBOUND: *Take the MLK Jr. Way Exit (after the Tukwila Exit). At the light, turn right onto Ryan Way and continue up the hill. *From there, follow the directions above.*

Kubota Garden

www.kubotagarden.org

Open daily from dawn to dusk, year-round
Dogs on-leash are welcome

- 20 acres, plus 27 acres of the adjoining Kubota Garden Natural Area
- No admission fee, but donations are welcome
- Picnicking permitted
- Portable restrooms
- PLANT SALES: Annual spring and fall plant sale, coordinated by the Kubota Garden Foundation
- STRUCTURES/FEATURES: Terrace Overlook, bronze entrance gate, white ornamental wall around the garden's perimeter, a bronze bell near the entrance, Japanese-style foot bridges, benches, arbors, large boulders, spring-fed ponds, creek, waterfalls, rock outcroppings, and a woodland trail. Garden space can be reserved for weddings.
- FUTURE ADDITIONS PLANNED: Visitor Center with restrooms, additional garden areas, completion of the ornamental wall to enclose the entire garden
- FEATURED PLANTS/COLLECTIONS: Japanese maples, weeping evergreens, (deodar cedars, pines, sequoias, and others), rhododendrons, azaleas, viburnums, camellias, ferns and other woodland plants, ground covers, ornamental grasses, bamboo, Norway Spruce, an umbrella pine, an old grand fir, a hedge of English yew, a grove of threadleaf cypress
- ACTIVITIES: Occasional special events, volunteer opportunities
- TOURS: Self-guided tours are welcome and do not require reservations. Free, public tours are offered the fourth Saturday of every month year-round. Private, group tours can be arranged by calling (206) 725-5060.
- NEARBY ATTRACTIONS: Boeing Museum of Flight, Bonsai Northwest (bonsai nursery and bonsai design classes at 5021 S. 144th St. in Tukwila), Fort Dent Park (6800 Fort Dent Way in Tukwila)
- NEARBY GARDENS: Highline SeaTac Botanical Garden, South Seattle College Arboretum, Seattle Chinese Garden

A bridge built by Landscape Horticulture students crosses a creek in one of the arboretum's woodland displays.

15 South Seattle College Arboretum
"An outdoor laboratory, classroom, and sanctuary"

Located on the South Seattle College campus in West Seattle, next to the Seattle Chinese Garden

6000 16th Ave. SW
Seattle, WA 98106
(206) 934-5300
www.southseattle.edu/arboretum

The South Seattle College (SSC) Arboretum is a five-acre outdoor classroom and wildlife sanctuary, located on a ridge overlooking downtown Seattle and Puget Sound's Elliott Bay. In 1978, the college established the arboretum in response to a petition by students in the college's Landscape Horticulture program.

The arboretum is open to the public for the purpose of "education, research, and public enjoyment" *(the SSC Arboretum website, 2014)*. Its design highlights woodland, native, herbaceous (non-woody), and unique plants, displayed among conifers and other evergreens. Conifers are exhibited in the *Coenesium Rock Garden* and *Milton Sutton Conifer Garden.* The *Sequoia Grove, Helen Sutton Rose Garden, Malmo Garden,* and *Erickson Garden* feature sequoias, roses, rhododendrons, birches, pines, and other plants. Along nearly every path, there are structures such as foot bridges, pergolas, raised display beds, and pavilions built by students in the college's Landscape Horticulture program. A large gazebo funded by the Federated Women's Club of West Seattle overlooks the adjacent Seattle Chinese Garden and downtown Seattle. The gazebo can be reserved for private events.

The *Coenesium Rock Garden* is a spectacular collection of dwarf conifers. The idea for the garden was conceived by the previous owner of a local conifer nursery and one of the college's Landscape Horticulture instructors. A stream designed by students flows through the displays. The rock garden was inducted into the Gardens for Peace program in 2010, an Atlanta-based, non-profit organization that fosters "respect for the environment and a climate of peace among all peoples" by linking gardens worldwide (*www.gardensfor peace.org, 2014).*

The branches of this weeping, blue Atlas cedar make a dramatic display along a path in the arboretum.

Scenes from the arboretum

The SSC Arboretum was given a Wildlife Sanctuary designation by the National Wildlife Federation and has been approved for "arboretum accreditation at Level 1" by ArbNet, (based at the Morton Arboretum near Chicago). Additionally, in 2013, the arboretum was designated an American Conifer Society Reference Garden.

The arboretum is open daily for year-round public enjoyment. Visitors often combine consecutive visits to the arboretum and the adjacent Seattle Chinese Garden. The *Puget Ridge Garden Center,* located beside the Chan Education Center near the arboretum entrance, sells plants and is open approximately one day per month during the growing season. Guided tours of the arboretum can be arranged on a limited basis. Visit the arboretum's web page on the South Seattle College website for more information.

DIRECTIONS FROM I-5 (North of Boeing field): Take the West Seattle Bridge, then go south on Delridge Way after crossing the bridge. At the third light, turn left onto SW Oregon, go up the hill, veer right onto 21st Ave. Go left onto Dawson, then right onto 16th Ave. Turn in to the north entrance of the SSC campus. The arboretum is on the left.

(South of Boeing field): Take Exit 158, cross over I-5, bear left onto Pacific Hwy S./Tukwila International Blvd. Take the ramp on the right to get onto W. Marginal Way/SR 99 headed north. Go under the SR 509 overpass and bear left onto Highland Pkwy. Continue up the hill, turn right onto SW Holden St., then right onto 16th Ave. Turn in to the north entrance of the SSC campus. The arboretum is on the left.

South Seattle College Arboretum

www.southseattle.edu/arboretum

Open daily from dawn to dusk, year-round
Dogs on-leash are welcome

- 5 acres
- No admission fee
- Picnicking permitted
- Restrooms available
- PLANT SALES: Plants and garden-related items are sold at the Puget Ridge Garden Center (beside the Landscape Horticulture building, near the arboretum's entrance) approximately one day per month
- STRUCTURES/FEATURES: Puget Ridge Garden Center, nursery, gazebo, pergolas, foot bridges, arbors, benches, pond. Most of the structures are built by the college's Landscape Horticulture students.
- FEATURED PLANTS/COLLECTIONS: Dwarf conifers, sequoias, rhododendrons, azaleas, heather, roses, dahlias, Japanese maples, drought-resistant plants, woodland plants, perennials
- ACTIVITIES: Horticulture classes offered at South Seattle College are open to hobby gardeners; wine tasting and related events are held at the Northwest Wine Academy's wine tasting room (located on the SSC campus, *www.nwwineacademy.com)*
- TOURS: Self-guided tours are welcome. Private tours for groups of 10 or more can be arranged through the arboretum coordinator.
- NEARBY ATTRACTIONS: Alki Beach waterfront park, shops and restaurants along California and Alaska streets in West Seattle, the Community Orchard of West Seattle *(listed under the "Community Connections" link on the SSC Arboretum website)*
- NEARBY GARDENS: Seattle Chinese Garden, Highline SeaTac Botanical Garden, Kubota Garden

This ornate gate in the Seattle Chinese Garden's Knowing the Spring Courtyard beckons visitors to explore the rest of the garden.

16　Seattle Chinese Garden
"A beautiful coming-together space"

Located on the South Seattle College campus in West Seattle, adjacent to the SSC Arboretum

6000 16th Ave. SW
Seattle, WA 98106
(206) 934-5219
www.seattlechinesegarden.org

The Seattle Chinese Garden is a beautiful example of Chinese garden design and architecture. The garden opened in February, 2011. It is being constructed in stages as a collaborative effort between architects and artisans from Seattle and its sister city, Chongqing, China, under the direction of the Seattle Chinese Garden Society. The completed garden will encompass five acres on a ridge and offer a vista of the Seattle skyline and Cascade Mountains.

This Sichuan-style garden is the only one of its kind outside China. The open-air *Pine and Plum Pavilion* was the first structure built in the garden, followed by the nearby 50 x 70-foot entry court named *Knowing the Spring Courtyard*. The courtyard's north gate is directly aligned with the Seattle Space Needle, which is visible through the gate. Both the courtyard and pavilion were built as a symbol of friendship between Seattle and Chongqing, China.

The garden's design incorporates the four elements of traditional Chinese gardens: water, stone, plants, and architecture. White walls surround the courtyard, and the intricate details of the columns, roof tiles, and windows are reflected in the courtyard's pond (pictured below). Rocks imported from China are stacked by the pond and in the courtyard's pine and rockery corner to represent mountains. Tall, bamboo stones, named for their resemblance to bamboo culms before they sprout, stand along one wall.

Near the courtyard, a pond and garden are home to water lilies, bamboo, and wild rose. The garden also features flowering plum trees, wintersweet, flowering dogwood, magnolias, nandina shrubs, azaleas, black bamboo, black pine, dawn redwood, and other plants native to China. The *Peony Garden* on an embankment outside the courtyard displays

Left: Wild rose and bamboo border the peaceful, Pine and Plum Garden. Right: Rocks imported from China create mountain vignettes in the garden's courtyard.

Above: Luoyang tree peony "Fragrant Jade." Right: Plum trees bloom at the garden in spring. Photos courtesy of the Seattle Chinese Garden.

more than 400 peonies, mostly tree peonies of two dozen varieties imported from China, that bloom in May. It is one of the largest public tree peony gardens on the West Coast.

The Seattle Chinese Garden is being created "as a means of celebrating Seattle's rich Chinese heritage and supporting the region's education, cultural, and business ties with greater China" *(the Seattle Chinese Garden website, 2014)*. As more funding becomes available, other features will be installed, including a teahouse on a lotus pond, a scholar's studio, an 85-foot viewing tower, a rushing stream, and pine and bamboo groves.

The garden offers an array of cultural activities for the public, including martial arts demonstrations, peony and bamboo festivals, a kite festival, and introductory classes on conversational Mandarin. A brochure is available in the courtyard for self-guided tours. Free, public tours are offered occasionally on Saturdays. Tours can also be arranged for groups by calling (206) 934-5219 at least two weeks in advance. The grounds can be rented for private events. See the Seattle Chinese Garden website for more information on the garden's development and special events.

Seattle Chinese Garden

www.seattlechinesegarden.org

The grounds are open daily from dawn to dusk, year-round.
The courtyard is open Tuesday through Sunday, 11:30am-5pm,
April through October.
(Check the garden's website for the courtyard's winter schedule)
Dogs on-leash are welcome

- 5 acres upon completion
- No admission fee, but donations are welcome
- Picnicking permitted
- Restrooms available in the Chan Education Center
- STRUCTURES/FEATURES: Sichuan-style courtyard, carved column bases, mosaic pavers, rocks imported from China, bamboo shoot rocks, reflecting pond, open-air pavilion, stream, ponds, benches, a large carp sculpture more than 100 years old, view of the Space Needle
- FUTURE ADDITIONS PLANNED: Teahouse on a lotus pond, scholar's studio, 85-foot viewing tower, rushing stream, pine and bamboo groves
- FEATURED PLANTS/COLLECTIONS: Flowering plum trees, wintersweet, dogwoods, dawn redwoods, tree peonies, black bamboo, magnolias, nandina shrubs, wild rose, ornamental grasses
- ACTIVITIES: Cultural events including peony and bamboo festivals and martial arts demonstrations. Classes are offered on Chinese cultural interests and the Mandarin language.
- TOURS: Self-guided tours are welcome and do not require reservations. Public tours are occasionally offered on Saturdays. Private tours for groups and individuals can be arranged by calling (206) 934-5219.
- NEARBY ATTRACTIONS: Alki Beach waterfront park, shops and restaurants along California and Alaska streets in West Seattle, the Community Orchard of West Seattle *(listed under the "Community Connections" link on the SSC Arboretum website)*
- NEARBY GARDENS: South Seattle College Arboretum, Highline SeaTac Botanical Garden, Kubota Garden

DIRECTIONS FROM I-5: Use the directions for the SSC Arboretum.

Beds of colorful annuals line the front of the Volunteer Park Conservatory in spring and summer.

17 Volunteer Park Conservatory
"A jewel of Victorian glasshouses"

Located at the north end of Volunteer Park, in Seattle's Capitol Hill neighborhood

1400 E. Galer St.
Seattle, WA 98112
(206) 684-4743
www.volunteerparkconservatory.org
www.seattle.gov/parks

The 6,300-square-foot Volunteer Park Conservatory is one of the few remaining Victorian glasshouses on the West Coast. The conservatory was manufactured by the Hitchings Company in New York at a cost of $5,000 and assembled in the park by the Seattle Parks Department. It opened its doors to the public in 1912 and celebrated its centennial in August, 2012.

Ephiphytes in the Bromeliad House

The structure is made of nearly 3,500 glass panes and five plant houses. Ponds, a stream, a waterfall, sand, rocks, and vignettes mimic a variety of plant habitats in the displays. In the *Bromeliad House*, visitors can view plants in the pineapple family, and epiphytes, such as tillandsias and staghorn ferns, that grow by attaching their roots to rough surfaces. The *Palm House* features palms, ginger plants, banana plants, and a large collection of orchids. In the *Fern House,* many species of ferns grow alongside other tropical plants such as cyads, Mexican breadfruit, hibiscus, papyrus, and carnivorous plants.

The *Cactus House* has cacti and other succulents such as a blue tequila agave, saguaro cactus, a 95-year-old jade plant that blooms in winter, and a potted collection of *Sansevieria* (a genus that includes snake plant and mother-in-law's tongue). Exhibits in the *Seasonal Display House* are rotated to highlight plants during the season in which they bloom: lilies, campanulas, and scented geraniums in spring; perennials in summer; chrysanthemums and hebes in fall; and azaleas and cineraria in winter. Wrought-iron tillandsia trees, a 35-panel stained glass canopy, and a half-circle lunette add to the building's elegance.

The conservatory is operated by the Seattle Parks Department in cooperation with The Friends of the Conservatory, a Board of Directors, and conservatory staff. The Friends mission is "to advocate and encourage

The Cactus House

The conservatory's climate-controlled environment creates ideal growing conditions for tropical plants.

preservation, public participation, and education with respect to the Volunteer Park Conservatory and its plant collection" *(the Volunteer Park Conservatory website, 2014)*. Proceeds from plant sales, events, and the Palm House Gift Shop help support the building's operations and maintenance. A plant guide is available for visitors who want to tour the displays independently. Guided tours can be arranged for groups by calling (206) 322-4112. For more information, visit the Volunteer Park Conservatory website.

DIRECTIONS FROM DIFFERENT EXITS ALONG I-5: **(From Exit 155/Olive Way):** *Go east on Olive Way. At the "T," turn left onto 15th Ave. In about a mile, turn left onto E. Galer St. and follow the signs to the conservatory.* **(From Exit 168S at Boylston/Roanoke St.):** *Turn left onto E. Roanoke, cross over the interstate, then merge into the right lane. Turn right at 10th Ave. (south), then left onto E. Prospect St. and left onto 14th Ave. Take the first exit in the roundabout (past the water tower and Asian Art Museum) and continue to the north end of the park.* **(From the south end of the arboretum):** *Turn right onto E. Madison St. Go several blocks, then turn right onto 15th Ave. Go several blocks on 15th Ave., then turn left onto Galer St. into Volunteer Park. Follow the signs to the conservatory.*

*See the conservatory's website for alternate directions.

Volunteer Park Conservatory

www.volunteerparkconservatory.org   www.seattle.gov/parks

Open Tuesday through Sunday, 10am-4pm, year-round

- 6,300-square-foot Victorian glasshouse, modeled after the Crystal Palace in London
- Admission fee. Admission on the first Thursday and first Saturday of every month is free.
- Picnicking permitted in the park, not in the conservatory
- Restrooms available in the park, not in the conservatory
- GIFT SHOP: Palm House Gift Shop and Resource Center, operated by The Friends of the Conservatory
- PLANT SALES: Annual May and September plant sale. Plants can also be purchased in the Palm House Gift Shop.
- STRUCTURES/FEATURES: Benches, sculptures, wrought-iron tillandsia trees, ponds, waterfall, 35-panel stained glass canopy, half-circle glass lunette above the main entrance, 3,426 panes of glass
- FEATURED PLANTS/COLLECTIONS: Bromeliads, palms, orchids, ferns, cacti, rare and unusual plants such as staghorn ferns and tillandsias, endangered plants, carnivorous plants, seasonal displays, annual flowers
- ACTIVITIES: Special events, holiday events, member events, summer camps, classes, exhibits, lectures, volunteer opportunities
- TOURS: Self-guided tours are welcome. Private, group tours can be arranged by calling (206) 322-4112 two weeks in advance.
- NEARBY ATTRACTIONS: Volunteer Park (the Asian Art Museum, a water tower with an observation deck 75 feet above the ground, bandstand, children's wading pool, play structure, and outdoor sculptures and monuments), Woodland Park Zoo, downtown Seattle, Olympic Sculpture Park (2901 Western Ave. near the Seattle waterfront)
- NEARBY GARDENS: Washington Park Arboretum, Seattle Japanese Garden, the Center for Urban Horticulture, Carl S. English Jr. Botanical Garden, Streissguth Garden (1640 Broadway E., on Capitol Hill), Woodland Park Rose Garden (adjacent to the Woodland Park Zoo at 750 N. 50th St.), Bellevue Botanical Garden

18   The University of Washington (UW) Botanic Gardens

Overview

In 2005, the University of Washington (UW) Botanic Gardens were founded "to unite the gardens and programs of the Washington Park Arboretum and the Center for Urban Horticulture" *(the University of Washington Botanic Gardens Fact Sheet, 2013)*. They are part of the university's School of Forest Resources, and both play a significant role in horticultural education and research. The Botanic Gardens' mission is "to sustain managed to natural ecosystems and the human spirit through plant research, display, and education" *(www.uwbotanicgardens.org)*. The gardens are located about five minutes from each other and are a popular destination for Washington residents and out-of-state visitors alike.

On the following pages, the *Washington Park Arboretum* and the *Center for Urban Horticulture* are listed separately since they are at different locations.

The *Seattle Japanese Garden* is located in the Washington Park Arboretum but is not operated by the University of Washington, so it is listed in its own section after the UW Botanic Gardens.

Flowering trees and shrubs form rows of color along the arboretum's Azalea Way in spring and summer.

UW Botanic Gardens:
Washington Park Arboretum
"A hidden gem on the shores of Lake Washington"

Located along Lake Washington in northeast Seattle

2300 Arboretum Drive
Seattle, WA 98112
(206) 543-8800
www.uwbotanicgardens.org
www.arboretumfoundation.org

The Washington Park Arboretum was established in 1934. Prior to its establishment, it was a park designed by the Olmsted Brothers landscape architecture firm from Massachusetts. Washington Park was used for picnics, hiking, bike riding, and other recreational activities. At that time, people traveled through the park on bicycles, horses, and horse-drawn carriages. A speedway for harness racing was even built in the park and used for about five years, until the arrival of automobiles in 1900. The track eventually became Azalea Way, the main pedestrian path through the arboretum.

Azalea Way is lined with azaleas, rhododendrons, flowering cherry trees, magnolias, dogwoods, lilacs, and viburnums. The trail begins at the *Graham Visitor Center* and traverses the hillside, connecting with trails that lead to other parts of the arboretum. The *Rhododendron Hybrid Garden* is a key feature along Azalea Way, displaying over 150 hybrid rhododendrons that mostly bloom from May through June.

The arboretum has been ranked as having one of the most important tree collections in North America, with well over 40,000 trees, shrubs, vines from more than 4,000 species and cultivars around the world, and over 240 state champion trees. The arboretum's other collections include camellias, hybrid rhododendrons, azaleas, magnolias, witch hazels, maples, and viburnums. If you visit in February, you might get to see Indian Plum shrubs in bloom. The arboretum is gorgeous any time of year, but most of the flowering trees and shrubs bloom between April and June.

The arboretum also has several theme gardens. The *Woodland Garden* contains one of the largest collections of Japanese maples in North America. Its two ponds sit amidst dogwoods, ferns, hellebores, and other woodland plants. The

Is it an azalea or a rhododendron? Azaleas are in the genus Rhododendron.

Wisteria vines create a purple canopy on the Visitor Center's veranda.

A perfect bloom forms on a tulip tree (left), and rows of rhododendrons line a path off of Azalea Way (right).

Witt Winter Garden showcases winter-blooming perennials and trees that provide color and characteristics for winter interest. The Winter Garden is a delight between November and March when much of the arboretum plant-life is dormant. The *Pacific Connections Garden* is being built in phases. It will cover about 12 acres, showcasing plants from five countries along the Pacific Ocean, including Cascadia and the Siskiyou Mountains (along the West Coast of the U.S.), Chile, New Zealand, Australia, and the Himalayas. When complete, visitors will see specimens such as a snow gum eucalyptus, monkey puzzle tree, gingko, and flax among other plants the garden will feature. The arboretum offers other areas to explore, including the *Pinetum Loop Trail* and the *Waterfront Trail* that skirts Duck Bay and leads to Marsh and Foster Islands. A walking map of the arboretum's trails and collections can be printed from the UW Botanic Gardens website.

The *Graham Visitor Center* was opened on the arboretum's 50th anniversary. The Visitor Center has a gift shop operated by the Arboretum Foundation, an information desk, exhibits, rental space, and restrooms. A display by the Hardy Fern Foundation showcases ferns and other Pacific Northwest plants in a bed outside the Visitor Center. The vines of a mature wisteria that cover the Visitor Center's veranda burst with purple blooms every June. The Visitor Center's adjacent event hall and courtyards can be rented for private events.

The arboretum covers 230 acres and is managed by a partnership between the City of Seattle and the University of Washington. When the university was established in 1895, an arboretum was already being envisioned for its campus. In 1898, the City of Seattle donated 50 oak trees and 50 honey locust trees to the university for Arbor Day, and in 1934, planning for the establishment of an arboretum began with an agreement between the city and university. The agreement spelled out how the land would be used, retaining the arboretum as a space to be enjoyed by the general public. In the partnership, the city owns the land and the university owns the plants. In 1935, the Arboretum Foundation was formed to provide financial support for the arboretum.

The arboretum offers numerous horticulture-related activities for the public, as well as school field trips, family ecology tours, research and volunteer opportunities, and college internships. Some activities require registration. A map and audio tours can be downloaded from the arboretum's website. Free guided walks are offered every Sunday for most of the year and do not require registration. Guided group tours can also be arranged by calling (206) 543-8801. For more information on the arboretum and its programs, visit the arboretum link on the UW Botanic Gardens website.

DIRECTIONS FROM I-5 (from downtown Seattle or north of Seattle): Take the SR 520 Exit east. Take the Montlake Blvd. Exit off of SR 520, then go straight onto Lake Washington Blvd. Follow the signs to the Graham Visitor Center.

FROM I-5 SOUTH OF SEATTLE (driving northbound): Take Exit 164A. Take the ramp onto 7th Ave., then turn right onto E. Madison St. Stay on Madison for about 2 miles, then turn left onto Lake Washington Blvd. and follow the signs to the Graham Visitor Center.

Washington Park Arboretum

www.uwbotanicgardens.org   www.arboretumfoundation.org

Open daily from dawn to dusk, year-round
The Graham Visitor Center is open 10am-4pm daily, year-round
Dogs on-leash are welcome

- 230 acres
- No admission fee
- Picnicking permitted
- Restrooms available
- GIFT SHOP: Located in the Graham Visitor Center. The gift shop is operated by Arboretum Foundation members.
- PLANT SALES: Plants are sold outside the Graham Visitor Center during open hours from April through October.
- STRUCTURES/FEATURES: Graham Visitor Center, native plant display beds, gazebo, benches, interpretive signs, plant identification tags, ponds, trails through the arboretum as well as along Union Bay. Wisteria Hall and courtyards (by the Visitor Center) can be rented.
- FEATURED PLANTS/COLLECTIONS: Magnolias, hybrid rhododendrons, azaleas, plants for winter gardens, woodland plants, witch hazels, viburnums, camellias, hollies, legumes (including wisteria), and plants from five countries along the Pacific Ocean
- ACTIVITIES: Numerous seasonal and special interest events, classes, workshops, member events, and volunteer opportunities. Master Gardener clinics are held in the Graham Visitor Center in summer.
- TOURS: Self-guided tours are welcome. Free, public tours are offered every Sunday from January through November. Audio tours can be downloaded from the UW Botanic Gardens' website.
- NEARBY ATTRACTIONS: Hiking trails on Foster Island, kayak rentals from the Aqua Verde Paddle Club, canoe rentals from the UW Waterfront Activity Center, Asian Art Museum (in Volunteer Park), Museum of History and Industry, Woodland Park Zoo, Volunteer Park, downtown Seattle, Bellevue
- NEARBY GARDENS: Seattle Japanese Garden (in the arboretum), Center for Urban Horticulture, Volunteer Park Conservatory, Streissguth Garden (1640 Broadway E. on Capitol Hill), Carl S. English Jr. Botanical Garden, Bellevue Botanical Garden, Woodland Park Rose Garden (adjacent to the Woodland Park Zoo at 750 N. 50th St.)

The Soest Herbaceous Display Garden at the University of Washington's Center for Urban Horticulture

UW Botanic Gardens:
Center for Urban Horticulture
"A place for learning and rejuvenation"
(Angie Narus, 2014)

Located on the University of Washington campus along Union Bay, north of the Washington Park Arboretum

3501 NE 41st St.
Seattle, WA 98112
(206) 543-8616
www.uwbotanicgardens.org

The Center for Urban Horticulture (CUH) consists of 16 acres of demonstration gardens and the 74-acre Union Bay Natural Area that the public can enjoy year-round. The Center opened in 1984 as a partnership between the University of Washington and the horticultural community, and became part of the UW Botanic Gardens in 2005. The Center was the

The Soest Herbaceous Display Garden's granite fountain is surrounded by demonstration beds showing different soil and light conditions.

"first institution in the United States to combine scientific research and teaching with outreach programs and library facilities available to horticultural scholars, landscape professionals, urban managers, horticultural societies, and the gardening public" *(Hinckley, Thomas M., abstract from The University of Washington and the College of Forest Resources' Center for Urban Horticulture: History and Programs).*

The CUH gardens consist of the *Soest Herbaceous Display Garden, Goodfellow Grove,* the *McVay Courtyard,* the *Seattle Garden Club's Fragrance Garden,* and the *Union Bay Natural Area.* The *Soest Herbaceous Display Garden* (pictured above) opened in 1998 with funds donated by Washington residents Orin and Althea Soest, who were supporters of horticulture. The Soest garden is comprised of eight display beds that demonstrate examples of approximately 280 annuals, bulbs, and ornamental grasses that do well in different soil and lighting conditions. The CUH's *McVay Courtyard* exhibits woody shrubs, bulbs, and ground covers that provide year-round interest. The *Fragrance Garden,* located by the Soest garden, offers a place for visitors to sit and enjoy fragrant plants around them. In the *Goodfellow Grove,* on the south side of the complex, a stroll through a grove of serviceberry trees demonstrates a landscape that changes from formal to natural (pictured on the following page). The grove also displays plants that are native to the Pacific Northwest.

The 74-acre *Union Bay Natural Area,* just beyond the Goodfellow Grove, was established on a previous landfill. Its four miles of shoreline and habitat for more than 200 bird species, as well as other wildlife, make it popular for bird-watching. The Union Bay Natural Area's trails are open to the public.

The buildings at the CUH house the *Miller Library* and an *herbarium*, and provide meeting space for garden and environmental groups, Master Gardener clinics, lectures, and educational programs. The Center is also the site for the Master Gardeners' huge spring and fall plant sales, and space can be rented for private functions. Visit the Center for Urban Horticulture link on the UW Botanic Gardens website for more information on the CUH gardens, buildings, and events.

DIRECTIONS FROM I-5: Take the SR 520 E. Exit, then the Montlake Blvd. Exit. Turn left at the light onto NE 45th St. Cross over the highway. Go past the UW stadium and turn right onto Mary Gates Memorial Way. The Center for Urban Horticulture and its gardens are on the right.

FROM THE ARBORETUM: Take Lake Washington Blvd. toward Montlake Blvd. Turn right onto NE 45th St. to cross over SR 520, then follow the directions from * above.

A spectacular bloom of Amelanchier x 'Grandiflora' (serviceberry trees) in the Goodfellow Grove.

Center for Urban Horticulture (CUH)

www.uwbotanicgardens.org

Open daily from dawn to dusk, year-round
Dogs on-leash are welcome

- 90 acres
- No admission fee
- Picnicking permitted
- Restrooms available in the CUH Merrill Hall during open hours
- PLANT SALES: Master Gardeners hold a large, annual plant sale on the grounds of the CUH in spring and fall
- STRUCTURES/FEATURES: Demonstration gardens surrounding a granite fountain, courtyard, fragrance garden, benches, Miller Library, herbarium, meeting rooms, grove of spring-flowering trees and native plants from the Pacific Northwest, trails through the Union Bay Natural Area on Foster Island.
- FEATURED PLANTS/COLLECTIONS: Herbaceous plants, ornamental grasses, flowering trees and shrubs, shade-loving plants, sun-loving plants, moisture-loving plants, drought-tolerant plants, serviceberry trees, native plants
- ACTIVITIES: Annual Garden Lovers Book Sale in spring, Children's Hour and other children's programs, Master Gardener clinics, symposiums, workshops, lectures, hiking and birdwatching on Foster Island. Meeting space and greenhouse space can be rented.
- TOURS: Self-guided tours only. Audio tours of the UW Botanic Gardens can be downloaded from the UW Botanic Gardens website.
- NEARBY ATTRACTIONS: Kayaking (kayaks can be rented from the Aqua Verde Paddle Club; canoes can be rented from the UW Waterfront Activity Center), Arboretum Waterfront Trail and Pinetum Loop Trail (in the Washington Park Arboretum), Asian Art Museum (in Volunteer Park), Museum of History and Industry, Woodland Park Zoo, downtown Seattle, Olympic Sculpture Park (2901 Western Ave. near the Seattle waterfront), Bellevue
- NEARBY GARDENS: Seattle Japanese Garden (in the arboretum), Washington Park Arboretum, Volunteer Park Conservatory, Streissguth Garden (1640 Broadway E. on Capitol Hill), Woodland Park Rose Garden (adjacent to the Woodland Park Zoo at 750 N. 50th St.), Carl S. English Jr. Botanical Garden, Bellevue Botanical Garden

The Seattle Japanese Garden's pond is full of life, including turtles, koi, frogs, and a heron that visits often.

19 Seattle Japanese Garden
"A compressed world of mountains, forests, lakes, rivers, tablelands, and a village"

Located in the Washington Park Arboretum

1075 Lake Washington Blvd. E.
Seattle, WA 98112
(206) 684-4725
www.seattlejapanesegarden.org
www.seattle.gov/parks

The idea for the Seattle Japanese Garden was conceived by the Arboretum Foundation nearly 30 years before the garden became a reality. In 1960, after receiving an anonymous monetary donation, the foundation hired world-renowned landscape designer Juki Iida to design the three-and-a-half-acre garden in the Washington Park Arboretum. Iida has designed more than 1,000 gardens and even received an honor from the Emperor of Japan for his achievements.

The Seattle Japanese Garden was designed to resemble scenery surrounding a Japanese village. Starting at the *Gate House Village,* one branch of the main path passes a mondo grass lawn, conifers, maples, rhododendrons, and a mixture of trees. Another branch of the path goes up to the garden's *Mountainside,* past a waterfall and an 11-tier *Pagoda,* down to the *Teahouse.* There are several stone lanterns along the paths. One of them weighing three-and-a-half tons was a gift from Kobe, Japan in 1957.

The garden's central pond, symbolizing a village lake, reflects the surrounding vegetation in its clear water. Visitors can watch koi, frogs, and turtles from the pond's banks, zig-zag bridge, and moon viewing platform. The garden's main path wraps around the pond, past a wisteria trellis, along an orchard of crabapple and cherry trees, and by the *Tea Garden* and *Teahouse* where traditional tea (Chado) demonstrations are held.

Several paths loop to other parts of the garden, and there are numerous places to get wide views of the landscape. Mosses, anemone, corsican mint, mondo grass and other ground covers grow under the plants and trees in the garden. Irises, forsythia, rhododendrons, azaleas, snowball bush, camellias, Andromeda (Lily of the Valley shrub), pines (including a 100-year-old Japanese pine), Japanese maples, wheel trees, bellflowers, and Japanese primroses are also among the garden's symphony of plants.

This stone bridge points the way to the garden's Mountainside and Teahouse.

This old Japanese maple greets visitors as they enter the garden.

Public tea ceremonies are held in the Teahouse.

Fall color frames the garden's central pond.

The Seattle Japanese Garden is operated by a partnership between the Seattle Parks Department and the Associated Recreation Council. The council schedules photography classes, horticulture classes, workshops, and special events at the garden such as Children's Day in May, the Japanese Star Festival in July, a Moon Viewing event in August, and a Respect for Elders event in September. Photography membership offers unique photo opportunities in the garden.

Maps for self-guided tours are available on the garden's website and at the garden's Gate House. Public tours led by Arboretum Foundation docents are offered on a limited basis during garden hours and included with general admission. Private tours for groups can be arranged by calling (206) 684-4275. A gift shop is located in the Gate House Village inside the garden entrance. See the Seattle Japanese Garden website or the Seattle Parks website for more information.

DIRECTIONS FROM I-5: Take the Exit for SR 520 East, then take the Montlake Blvd. Exit off of SR 520. Go straight at the traffic light onto Lake Washington Blvd. As you enter the arboretum, follow the signs to the Japanese Garden.

DRIVING NORTHBOUND, SOUTH OF SEATTLE, FROM I-5: Take Exit 164A. Take the ramp onto 7th Ave., then turn right onto E. Madison St. Stay on Madison St. for about 2 miles, then turn left onto Lake Washington Blvd. Follow Lake Washington Blvd. until you get to the Japanese Garden on the left.

Seattle Japanese Garden
www.seattlejapanesegarden.org   www.seattle.gov/parks

Opens at 10am, Tuesday through Sunday in March, October, and November. Open daily from April through September. Closing times vary throughout the year.

- 3.5 acres
- Admission fee
- Picnicking is not permitted in the garden, but picnic areas are available outside the garden's entrance and throughout Washington Park.
- Restrooms available in the garden's Gate House Village
- GIFT SHOP: Located in the garden's Gate House Village
- STRUCTURES/FEATURES: Gift Shop, Teahouse and Tea Garden, stone foot bridges, 11-tier pagoda, stone lanterns, central pond with koi and turtles, waterfall, stream, pavilion, trellis, boulders, benches, perimeter fence, numerous overlooks and sweeping views of the garden's central pond and surrounding landscape
- FEATURED PLANTS/COLLECTIONS: Japanese maples, rhododendrons, azaleas, crabapple and flowering cherry trees, magnolias, water lilies, Japanese irises, primroses, ground covers, ferns, wisteria, pines, Gingko bilobas (maidenhair trees)
- ACTIVITIES: Seasonal events including Children's Day, Japanese Star Festival, a Moon Viewing event, and a Respect for Elders day; tea ceremonies, photography classes, and workshops
- TOURS: A map for self-guided tours is available on the garden's website and at the garden's gatehouse. Public tours are offered daily with general admission when the garden is open. Private group tours can be arranged for an additional fee by calling (206) 684-4725.
- NEARBY ATTRACTIONS: Kayaking (kayaks can be rented from the Aqua Verde Paddle Club; canoes can be rented from the UW Waterfront Activity Center), Asian Art Museum (in Volunteer Park), Museum of History and Industry, Woodland Park Zoo, downtown Seattle, Bellevue
- NEARBY GARDENS: Center for Urban Horticulture, Volunteer Park Conservatory, Streissguth Garden (1640 Broadway E. on Capitol Hill), Carl S. English Jr. Botanical Garden (west), Bellevue Botanical Garden, Woodland Park Rose Garden (adjacent to the Woodland Park Zoo at 750 N. 50th St.)

The Bellevue Botanical Garden's award-winning perennial borders make an impressive display year-round. Photo by Rebecca Randall, courtesy of the Bellevue Botanical Garden.

20 Bellevue Botanical Garden
"A place to find beauty, solace, and renewal"

Located in Bellevue's Wilburton Hill Park, east of Seattle

12001 Main St.
Bellevue, WA 98005
(425) 452-2750
www.bellevuebotanical.org

The Bellevue Botanical Garden is 53 acres of display gardens, woodlands, meadows, and wetlands in Bellevue's 105-acre Wilburton Hill Park. The garden is dedicated to displaying "the best plants and gardening practices for healthy, beautiful Northwest Gardens *(the Bellevue Botanical Garden website, 2014)*. It is a classic example of green space that was spared development by the vision of the City of Bellevue and local citizens.

Spring in the garden

In the early 1980s, 100 acres of a wooded hillside in Bellevue's Wilburton neighborhood were set aside as the location for a government center. The proposed site surrounded the homestead of Cal and Harriet Shorts and a series of woodland trails that were used recreationally by local residents. Discussions between city officials and concerned community members changed the fate of the property, and it was instead developed into a city park.

The Bellevue Botanical Garden was established within the park on 7.5 acres donated by the Shorts. The garden was opened to the public in 1992 and has since been expanded to 53 acres. The Shorts became life members of the garden in 1994. The *Shorts House*, designed by architect Paul H. Kirk, has remained part of the garden and continues to be open to the public. The book *The Bellevue Botanical Garden: Celebrating the First 15 Years,* by Marty Wingate, gives a detailed look into the garden's history.

Many of the garden's display beds are planted and tended by volunteers from local community groups and businesses. The garden's award-winning *Perennial Borders*, maintained by the Northwest Perennial Alliance *(www. northwestperennialalliance.org),* showcase Great Plant Picks selections of "the best plants for healthy Northwest gardens and year-round color *(Nancy Kartes, Garden Manager).* The borders form rows on a terraced slope, making an impressive display any time of year. From there, the main path leads visitors past the Eastside Fuchsia Society's *Fuchsia Garden*, the Bellevue Utilities' *Waterwise Garden*, the Puget Sound Dahlia Association's *Dahlia Display*, the *Native Discovery Garden* maintained by the East Lake District of Garden Clubs, the *Shorts Ground Cover Garden, Rock Garden, Rhododendron Glen, Yao Garden*, and other displays.

The *Rhododendron Glen* showcases more than 50 different rhododendrons alongside hydrangeas, winter-blooming paperbush, flowering trees, and nearly 100 types of ferns planted by the Hardy Fern Foundation. The Japanese-inspired *Yao Garden*, installed with the help of Bellevue's sister city, Yao, Japan, is a blend of Northwest Pacific Rim influences and more than 60 plant species, including azaleas, viburnums, rhododendrons, and maples. The *Ravine Experience* is a favorite among kids, where a 150-foot suspension bridge gives visitors a unique view of the ravine below. The garden's new *Visitor Center Services and Education Center*, designed by Jim Olson of Olson Kundig Architects, house meeting rooms, restrooms, and the *Trillium Store*.

Heather, flowers, and ornamental grasses lead the way to the garden's Tateuchi Viewing Pavilion.

A camellia blooms beside the Tateuchi Viewing Pavilion.

The Ravine Experience's 150-foot suspension bridge

      The Bellevue Botanical Garden is managed by Bellevue Parks and Community Services in partnership with the Bellevue Botanical Garden Society and other horticulture groups. The society operates the garden's Trillium Store and sponsors events and seasonal celebrations, including the well-attended Garden d'Lights held in December, when visitors can enjoy plants and creatures shaped from thousands of tiny lights along the garden's paths. The Bellevue Botanical Garden is open year-round. Free, public tours are offered on weekends from late spring to early fall, and private group tours can be arranged by calling (425) 452-2750. A walking map and other information about the garden is available on the Bellevue Botanical Garden website.

      The Bellevue Botanical Garden is located in Wilburton Hill Park, which is part of a stellar park system along Bellevue's Lake-to-Lake Trail. See *www.ci.bellevue.wa.us/nature_trails.htm* for a list of the city's other parks, locations, and their websites.

<u>DIRECTIONS FROM I-405</u>: *Exit at NE 8th St. East, then turn right onto 120th Ave. (which becomes 1st St.). Go south about 3/4 mile, then turn left onto Main St. Go up the hill approximately 3 blocks to the garden.*

Bellevue Botanical Garden
www.bellevuebotanical.org

Open daily from dawn to dusk, year-round

- 52 acres
- No admission fee
- Picnicking permitted
- Restrooms available
- GIFT SHOP: Trillium Store, operated by the Bellevue Botanical Garden Society, located in the Visitor Services Building
- PLANT SALES: Annual spring, summer, and fall plant sales
- STRUCTURES/FEATURES: Visitor Services and Education Center complex, Tateuchi Viewing Pavilion, Shorts House, Sharps Cabin, 150-foot suspension bridge over a forested ravine, stone lanterns, outdoor sculptures, benches, ponds, streams, waterfall, boulders, overlooks, forest trails
- FEATURED PLANTS/COLLECTIONS: Rhododendrons, azaleas, maples, dahlias, flowering trees and shrubs, hardy fuchsia, spring bulbs, hydrangeas, ground covers, ferns, native plants
- ACTIVITIES: Special events such as concerts and art exhibits, annual Garden d'Lights holiday display and other seasonal celebrations, lectures and classes on horticulture topics, children and teen programs, volunteer opportunities
- TOURS: Self-guided tours are welcome. Free, public tours are offered on Saturdays and Sundays from April through October. Special tours for groups can be arranged by calling (425) 452-2750.
- NEARBY ATTRACTIONS: Wilburton Hill Park (ball fields, playground, picnic areas, zip line, and play structures at the intersection of 124th and Main St.), Lake-to-Lake Trail, Mercer Slough Nature Park, Bellevue Downtown Park, Bellevue Square, Bellevue Art Museum, Entai Beach Park (swimming, canoe and kayak rentals), Bellevue Skate Park, Kelsey Creek Farm
- NEARBY GARDENS: Washington Park Arboretum, Seattle Japanese Garden, Center for Urban Horticulture, Volunteer Park Conservatory, Woodland Park Rose Garden (adjacent to the Woodland Park Zoo at 750 N. 50th St., in Seattle)

Pieris (left), also known as Andromeda, and other flowering plants frame a walkway at the Carl S. English, Jr. Botanical Garden.

21 Carl S. English, Jr. Botanical Garden
"A horticultural treasure of the Pacific Northwest"

Located at the Chittenden Locks in Seattle's Ballard neighborhood (off of 54th St. and NW Market St.)

3015 NW 54th St.
Seattle, WA 98107
(206) 783-7059
www.nws.usace.army.mil (under the *Locations* and *Seattle District* links)
www.seattle.gov

The Carl S. English, Jr. Botanical Garden is the only public garden that is operated by the U.S. Army Corps of Engineers. The seven-acre garden is located on the north side of the Hiram M. Chittenden Locks that connect Lake Washington with Puget Sound in Northwest Seattle. The locks and ship canal are both listed on the National Register of Historic Places.

The locks were dedicated in 1917, and the grounds on the north side were designed with paved paths, grass lawns, trees, and plants donated by the Seattle Parks Department. Over the years, the Corps hired gardeners to maintain them. A trained botanist and pioneering horticulturist named Carl English, Jr. was the head gardener at the locks for 43 years. During his career, Carl transformed the sparsely-planted grounds into a beautiful English-style garden, surrounding the rolling lawns with trees from around the world and beds of flowers and shrubs. Many of the plants in the garden were started from seeds Carl obtained by trading with other horticulturists.

The garden features 3,500 varieties of interesting and colorful ornamental shrubs, flowers, and trees. Silktassel bush, pieris, osmanthus, flowering cherry trees, and rhododendrons grace the walkways. 200 varieties of roses, along with a plethora of spring bulbs such as daffodils, hyacinth, tulips, irises, and salvias brighten the formal *Rose Garden* and raised beds near the Administration Building. This garden boasts more than 500 species of trees from six continents, including windmill palms, oaks, horse chestnuts, dawn redwoods, buckeyes, weeping evergreens, Japanese pagoda trees, evergreen oaks, magnolias, alpine plants, unique native plants, a strong collection of trees from the Southern Hemisphere, and specimens of extremely rare plants.

Left: A canopy of cherry trees.
Right: Raised beds in the rose garden.

This 1916 photo shows new lawns, roads, and walkways on the grounds north of the Hiram M. Chittenden Locks before they became a botanical garden. The photo was taken looking westward toward the lock keeper's house (on the hill). Photo courtesy of the U.S. Army Corps of Engineers.

Several buildings share the grounds. The *Administration Building* is open for the public to view the building's architecture and historical photos. Its entrance is framed by two weeping Alaska yellow cedars that surpass the building's height. The *Visitor Center,* located in a separate building, has historical exhibits, information about the complex, and a gift shop. Plants can be purchased outside the Visitor Center between Mother's Day and Father's Day (mid-May to mid-June). The *Cavanaugh House* on the knoll west of the Visitor Center is a private residence and not open to the public.

In summer, the Carl S. English, Jr. Botanical Garden is a venue for outdoor concerts, children's theater productions, a classic car show, and the Greater Seattle Fuchsia Society's annual show. Special performances are held on July 4th and Labor Day in September. Visitors are welcome to take self-guided tours of the grounds. Many people combine a stroll through the garden with a tour of the locks and fish ladder viewing room, stopping in the Visitor Center and gift shop before leaving the complex. Free, guided tours of the garden and locks can be arranged by calling (206) 783-7059. See *www.nws.usace.army.mil* or *www.seattle.gov* for more information on the gardens, locks, ship canal, and fish ladder, as well as other civil works by the Army Corps of Engineers.

<u>DIRECTIONS FROM I-5</u>: Take Exit 169 to 45th St. Head west and merge onto 46th St., which becomes NW Market St. Go under the Aurora Ave. overpass. Bear left onto 54th St. and follow the signs to the locks complex.

Carl S. English, Jr. Botanical Garden

www.nws.usace.army.mil   www.seattle.gov

Open daily from dawn to dusk, year-round
Dogs on-leash are welcome

- 7 acres
- No admission fee
- Picnicking permitted
- Restrooms available
- GIFT SHOP: Located in the Visitor Center
- PLANT SALES: Plants can be purchased outside the Visitor Center between Mother's Day (mid-May) and Father's Day (mid-June)
- STRUCTURES/FEATURES: Historic buildings, nursery, Cavanaugh House (private residence), views of the locks and ship canal, arbors, formal rose garden, raised beds, paved walkways, wide lawns, benches, black iron fence and gates around the perimeter
- FEATURED PLANTS/COLLECTIONS: Roses, spring bulbs, unique flowers, palm trees, weeping cedars, snowball bush, magnolias, flowering cherries, Japanese maples, pieris, rhododendrons, more than 500 species of trees including specimens such as the wheel tree and European fan palm, trees from the Southern Hemisphere, rare plants
- ACTIVITIES: Outdoor summer concerts, special performances on July 4th and Labor Day in September, classic car show, children's theater productions, an annual fuchsia show
- TOURS: Self-guided tours are welcome. Guided tours of the locks and gardens can be arranged by calling (206) 783-7059.
- NEARBY ATTRACTIONS: Historic District along Ballard Ave., Golden Gardens Park (waterfront park at 8498 Seaview Place NW in Ballard), Nordic Heritage Museum (3014 NW 67th St.)
- NEARBY GARDENS: Volunteer Park Conservatory, Washington Park Arboretum, Seattle Japanese Garden (in the arboretum), Center for Urban Horticulture

Mature rhododendrons and trees, many of them as much as 100 years old, tower over the lawns at Dunn Gardens.

22 Dunn Gardens
"A historic treasure in Seattle"

Located in a quiet, Shoreline neighborhood, north of Seattle

13533 Northshire Rd. NW
Shoreline, WA 98177
(206) 362-0933
www.dunngardens.org

Anyone who is familiar with landscapes designed by the Olmsted Brothers can easily recognize the Olmsted signature in the Dunn Gardens. This beautiful, seven-and-a-half acre garden is located on what was originally undeveloped land that quietly overlooked Puget Sound and the Olympic Mountains.

The property was purchased in the early 1900s by Arthur Dunn and his family for a summer home. Arthur hired the Olmsted Brothers to design the landscaping, and they held true to their philosophy of retaining the property's natural features and terrain. Arthur contributed his own ideas to the plan by planting trees, flowering shrubs, and a variety of flowers along the wide lawns and paths. Flowers can be seen nearly everywhere in this garden, planted around trees and even in the lawn. One of the garden's most prominent features is the *Great Lawn* (pictured below), with crocuses growing in the grass, bordered by perennial beds, rhododendrons, deciduous trees, and evergreens. Mature sugar maples, oaks, rhododendrons, and camellias tower over the garden, forming a brightly-colored canvas most of the year. With its numerous flowering shrubs and deciduous trees, Dunn Gardens has spectacular color in spring and fall.

Arthur's son, Edward Dunn, was a respected garden writer and authority on Pacific Northwest native plants. Edward converted the garage building into a cottage as his own residence. Two other houses were built on the property by Dunn family members and have also remained part of the garden. Edward added the *Woodland Garden* near the cottage, planting fawn lilies, trilliums, hydrangeas, rhododendrons, and other plants he admired. He later established the E.B. Dunn Historic Garden Trust to preserve Dunn Gardens and other historically-significant gardens in the Northwest and educate the public about them. In 1994, Dunn Gardens was listed on the National Register of Historic Places.

Summer and fall color on the Great Lawn (left and right photos) and the Woodland Garden path (center). Left photo by Bob Findlay. Center photo by Beth Weir.

Above: Purple trillium along the path. Right: The curator's courtyard garden is ripe with color. Right photo by Connie Hokansen.

The Dunn Garden's curators, residing in Edward Dunn's former cottage, have created a spectacular *Courtyard Garden* (pictured above), which is a stop along the garden tour. Another 16 stations make up the tour, including the *Great Lawn, Croquet Lawn, Moss Garden, Pond Garden, Woodland Garden,* and *Upper Ravine Glade.*

Dunn Gardens can be visited by reserving space on a scheduled tour from April through October, and by registering to attend a lecture, workshop, the annual Fall Foliage Festival as a guest of a garden member, or any of the other special events or celebrations held at the garden. The garden is closed for the month of August. Visit the Dunn Gardens website for information on how to register for tours and events.

DIRECTIONS FROM I-5: Take Exit 175. Go west on 145th and cross over Hwy 99/Aurora Ave. and Greenwood Ave. Pass the Seattle Golf course. Turn left onto 3rd Ave., right onto NW 137th, and left onto Northshire Rd. NW. Go past three houses and make a right into the garden entrance marked by two brick pillars. Keep left and follow the green signs. Take the third right, then turn left into the parking area past the gray cottage.

Dunn Gardens
www.dunngardens.org

Can be visited through scheduled tours and special events,
April through October.
The garden is closed for the month of August.
Reservations are required for all visits

- 7.5 acres
- Admission fee
- Picnicking not permitted
- Restrooms available
- Gift-related items are sometimes available for purchase through donations during the garden's events.
- STRUCTURES/FEATURES: Garden curator's cottage (private residence) and courtyard garden, two other private residences (not open to the public), sculptures, stream, ponds, benches, container plants, wide lawns dotted with crocus flowers, outdoor sculptures
- FEATURED PLANTS/COLLECTIONS: Rhododendrons, crocuses, erythroniums (fawn lilies), trilliums, hydrangeas, cyclamen, ferns, water-loving plants, woodland plants, sugar maples, big leaf maples, Japanese maples, giant Himalayan lilies, heaths and heathers, flowering trees and shrubs
- ACTIVITIES: Annual Fall Foliage Festival (a member event), Mallets in Wonderland (a croquet event on the garden's Croquet Lawn held in August), seasonal events, other member events, classes, and workshops. *Centennial celebration in 2015*
- TOURS: Guided tours only. Tour sizes are limited and tend to fill quickly, so register early. Reservations are required for all visits. Check the garden's website for available tours and registration information.
- NEARBY ATTRACTIONS: Shoreline area parks and beaches (*www.cityofshoreline.com*)
- NEARBY GARDENS: Kruckeberg Botanic Garden, Elisabeth C. Miller Botanical Garden

Elisabeth and Pendleton Miller's former residence

23 Elisabeth C. Miller Botanical Garden
"The private garden of a beloved horticulturist"
(Angie Narus)

Located on Olympic Drive in The Highlands gated community of Shoreline, north of Seattle

Olympic Drive
Shoreline, WA 98177
(206) 362-8612
www.millergarden.org

The Elisabeth C. Miller Botanical Garden is the legacy of world-renowned and beloved horticulturist, Elisabeth Carey Miller (fondly known as "Betty"). In 1948, Elisabeth and her husband, Pendleton, purchased a three-acre parcel in the exclusive Highlands community north of Seattle. Architect Daniel Lamont built their house with red cedar siding and sandstone exterior walls, and Elisabeth designed and planted the garden.

Elisabeth focused on mixing native plants with non-native ones in a way that would make the design look natural rather than contrived. Her garden contains collections of alpines, *Rhododendron, Hepatica, Epimedium,* Ericaceae (the heath family), ground covers, and over 240 species and cultivars of ferns. The garden is now a leader in collecting and breeding hepaticas (colorful, early-blooming woodland perennials) in the garden's nursery located at the southwest corner of the property. All new plants go through a test period in the nursery before being added to the garden.

The quietness of this garden is immediately evident. Both the *Gully Garden* and plantings of Japanese maples, rhododendrons, other shrubs, and flowers provide a buffer between the house and road (pictured below). There is a balance of color and texture among each of the garden areas. Beds of flowers, ferns, and large plants border the lawn. A stone patio overlooks the garden's *Sunny Bank, Rockery, Alpine Terrace,* and *Lower Garden* filled with perennials, bulbs, spring flowers, and ground covers. The garden's curved path and stairs command a slow, easy pace. A deck in the Lower Garden overlooks Puget Sound with views of the distant Olympic Mountains.

The Gully Garden and other plantings form a buffer between the Miller House and the road. Photos by Richard A. Brown.

Plantings by the Miller House and in the Wild Garden demonstrate Betty's skill at mixing plants for a natural aesthetic.

Elisabeth was active in the horticulture community, was a member of over 25 horticulture organizations, and received numerous awards for her horticultural work. In 1996, Elisabeth, along with 12 other prominent Seattle women, founded the Northwest Horticultural Society and supported the formation of the Center for Urban Horticulture at the University of Washington. Elisabeth and Pendleton set up a charitable foundation, and the Elisabeth Miller Memorial Lecture and Great Plant Picks were two programs launched by grants awarded by the foundation. Great Plant Picks is a resource that recommends outstanding plants for the maritime Pacific Northwest. Over 900 plants selected by the program are listed on its website at *www.greatplantpicks.org.*

The Miller Garden is operated by a small staff that is overseen by a Board of Directors. The garden's mission is "to enhance horticulture in the tradition of Elisabeth Carey Miller by discovering, displaying, evaluating, and disseminating information about plants suitable for the Pacific Northwest" *(the Elisabeth C. Miller Botanical Garden website, 2014).* The garden sponsors the annual Elisabeth Miller Memorial Lecture and offers workshops led by horticulture professionals. The Miller Garden can be visited through scheduled tours and special events, April to October. Reservations are required. Tours fill up quickly (usually by mid-January), so register as early as possible for the coming year. See the Elisabeth Miller Botanical Garden website for more information.

Elisabeth C. Miller Botanical Garden
www.millergarden.org

Can be visited through scheduled tours and special events,
April to October
Reservations are required for all visits

- 3 acres
- No admission fee
- Picnicking not permitted
- Restrooms available
- PLANT SALES: Plants from the garden are often sold in the fall plant sale held at the Center for Urban Horticulture on the University of Washington campus
- STRUCTURES/FEATURES: Miller House, nursery, stone patio, stone stairs, stepping-stone paths, container plants, raised beds along the house, benches, wooden deck overlooking Puget Sound
- FEATURED PLANTS/COLLECTIONS: Alpine plants, drought-tolerant plants, epimediums, ericas, hepaticas, rhododendrons, more than 240 species and cultivars of ferns, more than 100 species of woodland plants, hellebores, black mondo grass, container plants, perennials, bulbs, spring ephemerals, ground covers, flowering shrubs and trees
- ACTIVITIES: Classes, workshops, annual Elisabeth Miller Memorial Lecture, other lectures, and internship opportunities. Registration is required.
- TOURS: Guided tours only. Tour sizes are limited and tend to fill up early in the year or sooner. Check the garden's website for available tour dates and registration information.
- NEARBY ATTRACTIONS: Shoreline area parks and beaches *(www. cityofshoreline.com)*
- NEARBY GARDENS: Dunn Gardens, Kruckeberg Botanic Garden

*Directions to the garden will be given upon registering for a tour or event.

The Kruckeberg Botanic Garden's courtyard is a tribute to Mareen Kruckeberg's love of container gardening.

24 Kruckeberg Botanic Garden

"Arthur and Mareen Kruckeberg, sharing their life's work with the community"

Located in Shoreline, north of Seattle

20312 15th Ave. NW
Shoreline, WA 98177
(206) 546-1281
www.kruckeberg.org

The Kruckeberg Botanic Garden is a collection of more than 2,500 native and exotic plants growing in a natural setting. The garden was started by Dr. Art and Mareen Kruckeberg when they purchased the farmhouse and four-acre lot in 1958. It was their home for more than 50 years. Art was a botanist, collector, and professor at the University of Washington; Mareen was a horticulturist and artist. Both were active in the horticulture community and helped establish several horticultural societies, including the Hardy Fern Foundation and the Washington Native Plant Society.

Mareen was interested in plant propagation and garden design. On Mother's Day, she would open the garden to visitors to sell plants she had propagated. She later opened the *MsK Rare and Native Plant Nursery* at the garden. The nursery is located in the *Upper Garden*, along with the Kruckeberg farmhouse, caretaker's cottage, and courtyard. Some of Mareen's prized plant containers are displayed outside the cottage, and additional potted containers line the courtyard.

Dr. Art Kruckeberg's main interest was in collecting and growing trees from around the world. The majority of his collection is showcased with groupings of plants and trees mulched with bark, and rare specimens of trees displayed in serpentine, or rock beds, in the *Lower Garden*. A chokecherry, tanbark oak (mutant form), and giant sequoia are a few of the trees to admire in the collection, along with some of the largest and rarest trees in Washington State. Dr. Kruckeberg turned 95 in 2015, still residing in the farmhouse.

Flowering plants such as lewisias, fawn lilies, trilliums, rhododendrons, and dogwoods add to the garden's palette, while pops of color emerge along the path in early spring. A new *Native Plant Demonstration Garden* in the Lower Garden will feature forest plants, a prairie, fern grotto, wetland area, and a garden of white flowering plants. Sculptures can also be enjoyed throughout the garden, including the large, natural sculpture titled "Wood Wave" that

This 12'x10'x8' interactive sculpture titled "Wood Wave," by artist Bruce Johnson, was installed at the garden in 2013. Photo by Brianne Zorn, courtesy of the Kruckeberg Botanic Garden.

Lewisia cotyledon (left), fawn lilies (center), and yellow blooms on a Parrot-iopsis tree (right). Left photo by Vicki Demetrie. Center photo courtesy of Kruckeberg Botanic Garden.

was installed in 2013, and temporary exhibits of student and professional art.

Native plants and hardy exotics grown in the garden are sold at the on-site nursery operated by the Kruckeberg Botanic Garden Foundation. The foundation is dedicated to "sustaining the Kruckeberg legacy by demonstrating how plants enrich our lives and our community" *(the Kruckeberg Botanic Garden website, 2014)*. Foundation volunteers help maintain the garden, offer educational programs, and continue Mareen's tradition of holding an annual plant sale on Mother's Day.

The Kruckeberg Botanic Garden is now owned by the City of Shoreline and has a city park designation. Plant sales, an annual Easter Egg Hunt, a Rake and Bake volunteer work party, and workshops are held throughout the year. Programs such as Garden Tots and botanical art classes are also offered. Guided public tours are offered on many Saturdays, and private group tours can be arranged by contacting *tours@ kruckeberg.org* or by calling (206) 546-1281. The garden is open to the public year-round. Visit the Kruckeberg Botanic Garden website for more information on the garden and its history.

DIRECTIONS FROM I-5: *Take Exit 176 onto 175th St. Go west. Cross Aurora Ave./Hwy 99. Turn right onto Fremont Ave., then left (west) onto 185th St. Continue on 185th/Richmond Beach Rd. Turn right (north) onto 15th Ave. NW. The garden is about 1/2 mile up the hill.*

Kruckeberg Botanic Garden
www.kruckeberg.org

The garden and nursery are open Friday, Saturday, and Sunday,
10am-5pm, year-round (shorter hours in winter).
Dogs on-leash are welcome

- 4 acres
- No admission fee, but donations are accepted
- Picnicking permitted
- Restrooms available
- PLANT SALES: Plants are sold at the on-site MsK Rare and Native Plant Nursery during garden hours and special plant sales. The nursery is operated by the Kruckeberg Botanic Garden Foundation.
- STRUCTURES/FEATURES: Kruckeberg farmhouse (information area, offices, and restrooms for garden guests are on the lower level), caretaker's cottage (private residence), propagation house, courtyard with benches and container plants, Wood Wave interactive sculpture and other outdoor sculptures
- FEATURED PLANTS/COLLECTIONS: Over 2,500 plants including rhododendrons, camellias, oaks, and ferns; unusual plants, exotic trees, lewisias, fawn lilies, trilliums, plants featured in the white garden, native plants, and container plantings
- ACTIVITIES: Seasonal events for children and adults including an annual Easter Egg Hunt, Garden Tots program, horticulture classes, and botanical art workshops; school field trips, member events, volunteer work parties
- TOURS: Self-guided tours are welcome and do not require reservations. Docent-led tours are frequently offered on weekends and require registration. Group tours can be arranged by calling (206) 546-1281 or emailing *tours@kruckeberg.org*. Some tours require a fee.
- NEARBY ATTRACTIONS: Shoreline area parks and beaches *(www.cityofshoreline.com)*
- NEARBY GARDENS: Elisabeth C. Miller Botanical Garden, Dunn Gardens

"The Entry Gateway," designed by artists David Little and George Lewis, topped with an arbor by artist Rex Lukinich, marks the entrance to the arboretum.

25 Evergreen Arboretum & Gardens
"Snohomish County's treasure"

Located in Legion Park, north of the Everett Marina

145 Alverson Blvd.
Everett, WA 98201
(425) 257-8597
www.evergreenarboretum.com

The Evergreen Arboretum and Gardens is a place that has truly embraced change. The arboretum was founded by the Everett Garden Club on Arbor Day, 1963. It was initially developed on land donated by the Everett Parks Department that was adjacent to the American Legion Memorial Golf Course and Legion Park. When the golf course was redesigned in the 1970s, the arboretum was moved to a smaller, three-and-a-half-acre site in the park.

The new location paved the way for the arboretum to take on a different role, focusing on plants ideal for residential spaces. A pin oak that was the first tree planted at the original site still stands at the 10th hole on the golf course. In 2013, a second pin oak was planted to commemorate the arboretum's 50th anniversary.

The mission of the arboretum and gardens is to "spread understanding and enjoyment related to the plant world by providing an easily accessible public garden dedicated to study, relaxation, and inspiration" *(the Evergreen Arboretum and Gardens website, 2014)*. A wide variety of flowers, shrubs and trees are displayed throughout the arboretum in 10 theme gardens, connected by paths of pervious material.

The *Conifer Garden* was installed first. Other areas include the *Japanese Maple Grove* showcasing 25 cultivars of maples, the *Rock Garden* below the *Viewing Mound,* the *Northwest Native Plant Trail, Rain Garden, Woodland Garden, Urban Tree Walk* showing examples of trees and shrubs suitable for small garden spaces, and the 200-foot-long *Demonstration Perennial Border*. The Perennial Border is maintained by the Snohomish County Master Gardeners and features plants well-suited for the Pacific Northwest climate. The final phase of the arboretum's development includes a bog garden and an expansion to the Native Plant Trail, designed by landscape architecture students from the University of Washington.

Left: The Master Gardener's Demonstration Perennial Border. Center: A pervious path of crushed glass weaves its way through the garden areas. Right: Fritillaria flowers in the Perennial Border.

The Conifer Garden

Outdoor art is an important part of the Evergreen Arboretum and Gardens. Art from both a permanent collection by noted Northwest artists and a rotating selection from the Everett Cultural Arts Department is exhibited among the plants. The entrance archway and a water feature titled *Fibonacci* (located on the *Viewing Mound)* are two fascinating examples in the arboretum's permanent art collection.

The arboretum is open daily, year-round. It is maintained by a joint effort between Everett Parks and Recreation and the Evergreen Arboretum and Garden Foundation, with help from numerous volunteers and the Snohomish County Master Gardeners. The foundation raises funds for the arboretum through events and an annual plant sale. Free workshops on gardening topics are held at the arboretum monthly. Visitors can tour the garden on their own, and private tours can be arranged for groups by calling (425) 257-8597. Dogs on-leash are welcome. See the Evergreen Arboretum and Garden website for more information.

DIRECTIONS FROM I-5: Take the exit for 529 S. and E. Marine View Drive (Exit 195 northbound and Exit 198 southbound). Go past the Legion Park Golf Course entrance. Turn left onto Alverson Blvd., then take the next left into Legion Park. Turn right when entering the parking lot. The arboretum is at the far end of the lot.

Evergreen Arboretum & Gardens
www.evergreenarboretum.com

Open daily from dawn to dusk, year-round
Dogs on-leash are welcome

- 3.5 acres
- No admission fee
- Picnicking permitted
- Restrooms available
- PLANT SALES: Annual plant sale in June, held by the Evergreen Arboretum and Gardens Foundation
- STRUCTURES/FEATURES: Horticulture building, trellises, arbors, pavilion, benches, sculpture collection, rotating outdoor art exhibit, animal and botanical prints stamped in the walkways, plant identification plaques
- FEATURED PLANTS/COLLECTIONS: Conifers, perennials, ferns, rhododendrons, native and woodland plants, small trees suitable for urban landscapes, alpine plants, Japanese maples, ornamental grasses, ground covers
- ACTIVITIES: Gardens of Merit Tour (held every other year), free workshops on gardening topics, volunteer work parties
- TOURS: Self-guided tours are welcome. Guided group tours can be arranged by calling (425) 257-8597.
- NEARBY ATTRACTIONS: American Legion Memorial Golf Course and adjacent Legion Memorial Park, Everett Marina (shops, Sunday Farmers' Market, and a four-mile paved waterfront pedestrian walk), Marina Beach Park on Admiral Way, Mukilteo Park and Lighthouse
- NEARBY GARDENS: Meerkerk Gardens on Whidbey Island (20 minutes to the island by ferry), Nishiyama Japanese Garden on the Everett Community College Campus (open when college classes are in session; *www.everettcc.edu/programs/communications/nbi/ nishiyama-japanese-garden)*

Visitors to Meerkerk Gardens are greeted by an English-style gate-house and an array of flowering plants. Photo by Melanie Hester.

26 Meerkerk Gardens
"A peaceful, woodland garden"

Located on Whidbey Island in North Puget Sound

3531 Meerkerk Lane
Greenbank, WA 98253
(360) 679-1912
www.meerkerkgardens.org

Meerkerk Gardens on Whidbey Island is a combination of a serene, 10-acre garden surrounded by 43 acres of forest preserve and over five miles of trails. The founders, Max and Ann Meerkerk, were inspired by Washington's native flower, the Pacific Rhododendron, when they began to develop the garden at their Whidbey Island home in 1961.

Ann was a hybridizer of rhododendrons and an active member of the Washington Park Arboretum and the Seattle Chapter of the American Rhododendron Society. She was also an artist and weaver, and raised sheep for wool. One of Ann's former sheep sheds is now used for selling plants in the garden's Rhododendron Specialty Nursery. The Meerkerk's former house is on the property but currently not open to the public.

Ann and Max planted their first five acres as an arboretum, known as the *Secret Garden,* with trees and plants they acquired from Northwest hybridizers and on their trips to England and Asia. Much of the garden's design was influenced by Max's time in Asia and by the Rothschild's Exbury Gardens in England, as evident in Meerkerk's Asian-themed garden and the design of the gatehouse. The garden paths take visitors through a full 10 acres that include the *Secret Garden, Asian Garden, Hall Garden, Rock Garden, Meditation Garden,* and the *Hybridizer's Garden.* Other paths cut through a portion of the surrounding woodland and a grove of big leaf rhododendrons. The garden areas are marked by decorative, hand carved signs (pictured below).

Meerkerk Gardens is home to both native and exotic specimens, including a 90-year-old rhododendron, fragrant rhododendrons, an empress tree, a diamond bark maple, and a monkey puzzle tree given to Ann at the Seattle World's Fair. Brilliant rhododendrons, azaleas, magnolias, dahlias, lilies, and a multitude of other plants create a spectrum of

Two of Meerkerk Gardens' hand carved directional signs. The sign in the left photo, made by volunteer Pat McVay, marks the turnoff at the corner of Resort Rd. and Hwy 525. Left photo by Joan Bell.

Daffodils and big leaf rhododendrons bloom along the garden trails.

color. A sustainable method if irrigation is used in the garden by collecting water in a bioswale and three ponds, then pumping it to the garden areas.

In 1979, Ann bequeathed the garden to the Seattle Rhododendron Society whose mission is "to care for the Meerkerk Gardens as a peaceful, woodland garden with an emphasis on rhododendrons and companion plants" *(the Meerkerk Gardens website, 2014)*. The garden was opened to the public in 2002 and is now managed by a volunteer Board of Directors. The board members, the Friends of Meerkerk, a team of volunteers, the Island County Master Gardeners, and local garden clubs contribute many hours to maintain and improve the garden.

The garden's on-site *Rhododendron Specialty Nursery* sells rhododendrons and companion plants from around the world. The nursery is open during garden events, plant sales, and garden hours in spring. The nursery has a plant sale every year at the end of March and another one at the end of the season over Labor Day weekend in September. The garden also has an on-site *Rhododendron Genetic Library* that has cataloged more than 150 years of combined hybridizing research.

Meerkerk Gardens holds several annual events, including a Mother's Day Concert, Wine and Rhodies Evening, Fall Garden Fest, Bluegrass Concert, Classic Auto Show, a Meerkerk Magic fairy doll making class, a fairy house building class, and workshops. Botany Adventure Nature Tours are offered for school groups in spring, and guided, horticultural tours can be arranged for groups of ten or more by calling (360) 678-1912 or at *meerkerk@whidbey.net*. The garden is open to the public daily, and dogs on-leash are welcome.

In 2013, a commemorative license plate displaying the Washington State flower was specially designed to help benefit Meerkerk Gardens and fund grants offered by the garden to horticultural organizations statewide. Visit the Meerkerk Gardens website for more information about the garden, its events, and the license plate.

DIRECTIONS: *Whidbey Island can be reached by the Mukilteo/Clinton ferry and the Port Townsend/Keystone ferry, and by Hwy 20 on the north end of the island. On Whidbey Island, follow Hwy 525 to Resort Rd. on the south end of the island (15 miles north of the Mukilteo/Clinton ferry terminal and 2 miles south of Greenbank). Go east on Resort Rd. and follow it for about 1/2 mile to the Meerkerk Gardens entrance. A hand carved sign for Meerkerk Gardens marks the turnoff at Hwy 525 and Resort Rd.*

Left: April inside the gatehouse. Right: A trail in bloom. Photos by Joan Bell.

Meerkerk Gardens
www.meerkerkgardens.org

Open daily 9am-4pm, year-round
Dogs on-leash are welcome

- 10 acres of gardens surrounded by 43 acres of forest preserve and over five miles of nature trails
- Admission fee. On plant sale days, admission is free.
- Picnicking permitted
- Restrooms available
- PLANT SALES: Annual spring, summer, and fall plant sale. The Rhododendron Specialty Nursery is open during plant sales, as well as during the garden's regular hours in spring and by appointment.
- STRUCTURES/FEATURES: English-style Gatehouse, Rhododendron Genetic Library, volunteer cottage and office, plant sale shed and greenhouse, the former Meerkerk residence, outdoor sculptures, outdoor concert pavilion, benches, hand carved signs
- FEATURED PLANTS/COLLECTIONS: Rhododendrons, azaleas, companion plants, spring bulbs, woodland plants, native and exotic trees
- ACTIVITIES: Mother's Day concert, Wine and Rhodies Evening, Fall Garden Fest, Bluegrass Concert, Classic Auto Show, Meerkerk Magic fairy doll making class, fairy house building class, workshops, volunteer opportunities
- TOURS: Self-guided tours are welcome and do not require reservations. Group tours of ten or more, and Botany Adventure Youth Tours for school groups in grades 3 through 5, can be arranged by calling (360) 678-1912.
- NEARBY ATTRACTIONS: Deception Pass and Dugulaia State Park on North Whidbey Island, Fort Casey and Admiralty Head Lighthouse in Keystone State Park, Whidbey Island towns, vineyards and wineries
- NEARBY GARDENS: Evergreen Arboretum and Gardens in Everett (on the mainland, north of Seattle; approximately 20 minutes by ferry and another 10 minutes by car)

Central and Eastern Washington

In Central and Eastern Washington, fields of golden wheat can be seen for miles, and the flatter terrain allows for wide views of orchards, vineyards, farms, and river valleys. The hot summers and lack of rain are accommodated by irrigation, allowing gardeners to grow flowers, shrubs, deciduous trees, fruit trees, drought-tolerant plants, and perennials that are able to withstand the extreme temperature changes. Each garden on the following pages has a different plant palette based on the growing conditions for that region. They are listed geographically to form a driving loop between Wenatchee, Yakima, Pullman, and Spokane. Above photo by Meghan Pasquariello.

Cascading waterfalls and crystal-clear pools at Ohme Gardens look as if they were placed there by nature.

27 Ohme Gardens
"An alpine wonderland" (Mike Short, Garden Manager)

Located on a bluff north of Wenatchee, overlooking the Columbia River

3327 Ohme Rd.
Wenatchee, WA 98801
(509) 662-5785
www.ohmegardens.com

The nationally-acclaimed Ohme Gardens (pronounced "oh-mee") has been called a labor of love. The garden covers nine acres high on a rugged bluff overlooking the Columbia River, a few minutes outside Wenatchee. Its slopes are graced with wildflowers, ground covers, woodland plants, tall evergreens, natural-looking waterfalls and ponds, and nearly a mile of stone paths.

Ohme Gardens was designed solely by the imagination

and intuition of Herman and Ruth Ohme. When Herman purchased the property in 1929, it consisted of a house, a five-acre apple orchard, and a rocky, sagebrush-covered bluff. Herman cleared the land, planted trees that are still in the garden today, and built a small rock garden with rocks he hauled up the hill in his car. In 1930, Herman married Ruth Orcutt. He and Ruth would often stand on the bluff and dream of living in a house surrounded by alpine meadows, reflecting pools, and tall evergreens.

Over the next 42 years, the Ohmes worked toward that dream, building a garden with little more than picks, shovels, sledge hammers, buckets, an army stretcher for hauling rocks, and their own hands. They dug up small trees and ferns in the mountains, then drove them back to their property on the rumble seat and running boards of their Studebaker Coupe. They also took flagstone from the banks of the Columbia River and the surrounding hills to make paths, benches, and pools. Little did they realize their alpine wonderland would one day become an attraction admired by people worldwide.

Left: The garden's stone paths lead to open views of the valley and distant mountains. Right: Most of the evergreens in the garden are over 80 years old.

The ponds that the Ohmes installed resemble natural, alpine lakes.

Herman and Ruth let the terrain and their own creativity dictate the garden's design. They planted lavender, phlox, columbines, asters, bellflowers, violets, sedums, thyme, *Lewisiopsis tweedyi* (found only in the Eastern Cascades), and other alpine and native plants along the garden's stone paths traversing the bluff's rolling slopes. The garden took shape, and features such as *Cactus Point, Twin Pools, Hidden Pool, Sylvan Pool, Enchantment Falls, Fernery, Decision Point Falls, Wedding Path,* and *Hook Lawn* began to change the look of the rocky bluff. Herman also built a wishing well, secret alcoves, wooden structures, a stone fireplace, and stone benches in the garden along the garden's stone paths. The log pavilion dubbed *Vista House* sits on the bluff's highest point, offering a breathtaking view of the river and mountains.

It took 10 years to develop the first two acres of the garden. As the hillside was transformed, curious locals came up to see what was taking shape. When public interest piqued, Herman agreed to open the garden for a small fee. Herman and Ruth eventually sold the garden to their son, Gordon, who continued to enhance it. In 1991, Gordon sold it to the State of Washington, and ownership of the garden was later transferred to Chelan County.

In 2008, the Ohme Gardens Friends Society was formed "to perpetuate Ohme Gardens for the enjoyment and education of all visitors" *(the Ohme Gardens website, 2014)*. The society raises funds for garden projects and helps with the garden's planting and maintenance tasks. The Lions Club funded a wheelchair-accessible trail leading to the *Sunken Lawn,* and the irrigation system was recently replaced. Plans are also being made to use one of the garden's wooden structures as an educational interpretive center. The book, *Ohme Gardens: Alpine Wonderland,* by Mike Short, explains the garden's history in text and photos.

Ohme Gardens offers annual events for the public to enjoy, including a Mother's Day Tea, a Wine and Food Gala, summer concert series, and outdoor theater productions. Visitors are welcome to explore the wonders of this garden on their own. Walking maps are provided at the entrance station. Group tours can be arranged by calling (509) 662-5785, and garden space can be rented for weddings. Plants propagated at the garden, including Ohme Gardens Thyme, are sold by the entrance station throughout the garden's open season. See the Ohme Gardens website for more information.

DIRECTIONS FROM SR 97A: (Located near the junction of US 2 and 97A). Turn off 97A onto Easy St. (on the north side of 97A). Turn right onto Ohme Gardens Rd., then left onto Ohme Rd. Follow the signs up the hill to the garden.

Wildflowers originally planted by the Ohmes now dot the hillside by the garden's streams, pools, and stone paths.

Ohme Gardens
www.ohmegardens.com

Open daily from 9am-6pm, April 15 to October 15
(Open until 7pm in summer months)

- 9 acres
- Admission fee
- Picnicking permitted
- Restrooms available
- GIFT SHOP: A small selection of gift items and books are for sale in the entrance station
- PLANT SALES: Plants are sold outside the entrance station during open hours
- STRUCTURES/FEATURES: Rustic pavilions (Totem Pole Lodge, Vista House, and Ox Yoke Lodge), outdoor stone fireplace, stone benches, waterfalls, reflecting pools, a stone wishing well, rock outcroppings, stone paths and stairs, large boulders, sweeping views of the Columbia River and distant mountains
- FEATURED PLANTS/COLLECTIONS: Phlox, sedums, lewisia, columbine, asters, paintbrush, globemallow, daises, bellflowers, other alpine plants, woodland and native plants, dogwood, evergreen trees, Ohme Gardens Thyme (propagated at the garden)
- ACTIVITIES: Mother's Day Tea, Wine and Food Gala, outdoor theater productions, summer concert series, outdoor yoga classes, nature photography classes, volunteer opportunities
- TOURS: Self-guided tours are welcome and do not require reservations. Private, group tours can be arranged by calling (509) 662-5785. Garden space can be rented for weddings.
- NEARBY ATTRACTIONS: Downtown Wenatchee, Pybus Public Market events (3 N. Worthen in Wenatchee), Apple Capital Loop Trail, Rocky Reach Dam and Arboretum, Lake Entiat on the Columbia River, Lake Chelan, Leavenworth, hiking trails in Wenatchee National Forest, local produced stands, wineries, vineyards, Cascade Loop scenic highway (www.cascadeloop.com)

Fall color envelopes the pagoda near the Yakima Area Arboretum's Joyful Garden. Photo by Colleen Adams-Schuppe.

28 Yakima Area Arboretum
"A living plant museum"

Located in the heart of Yakima, along the Yakima River

1401 Arboretum Drive
Yakima, WA 98901
(509) 248-7337
www.ahtrees.org

The 46-acre Yakima Area Arboretum sits beside the Yakima River in Central Washington. The arboretum was established in 1967 by the Central District of the Washington State Federation of Garden Clubs as a living tree and plant museum.

The arboretum is comprised of 32 acres of irrigated land and 12 acres of natural area. Its location by the river forms a narrow border of riparian habitat within the shrub-steppe zone of Central Washington, making it an ideal spot for birdwatching.

Gardeners in this region irrigate to make up for the lack of rainfall, allowing them to grow many plants and trees that might not grow as well on the western side of the mountains. The Yakima Area Arboretum is no exception. The arboretum displays more than 1,000 native, adapted, and exotic trees, flowering plants, grasses, and shrubs in display beds, groves, and groupings. Its groves of nut trees, flowering cherries, and crabapples put on a showy display in spring and fall. The crabapple collection of more than 50 cultivars is one of the largest in the Pacific Northwest. The arboretum's other collections consist of conifers, hawthorns, sequoias, beeches, and viburnums.

The arboretum has more than a dozen themed areas which include the *Rose Garden, Yellow Garden, Rock Border Garden, Kara Kondo Dryland Garden, Xeric Garden Demonstration Site, Organic Vegetable Demonstration Garden, Nursery, Joyful Garden, Pagoda Garden, Carlson Butterfly Garden,* and the *Iris Display Garden,* each demonstrating sound arboricultural practices and sustainable gardening methods. Flowing drifts of lavender, irises, English daisies, and other flowers are planted along the arboretum's perimeter.

The *Rose Garden* exhibits more than 300 roses surrounding a granite fountain and gazebo, and is an appealing location for wedding photography. Some of the arboretum's

The Kara Kondo Dryland Garden (above) and Joyful Garden (right). Above photo by Collen Adams-Schuppe.

The Rose Garden

newest additions include the *Demonstration Backyard Wildlife Garden, Edible Shrub Bed,* and *Bee Apiary.*

The arboretum's Japanese-inspired *Joyful Garden* is made up of pines, woodland plants, a pond, foot bridges, and boulders in an open setting. The garden was designed by landscape architect Jack Takayama and installed in 1976 with the help of the Yakima community and Yoshio Hata from the Japanese community of Wapato, Washington. Flowering cherry trees and the Joyful Garden's hand carved lantern were gifts from the mayor of Yakima's sister city, Itayanagi, Japan.

The arboretum's *Jewett Interpretive Center* was built with a donation from Don and Helen Jewett in 1992. It houses the Tree House Museum Store, as well as an interpretive display on the Heritage of Trees in Yakima Valley, a reference library, solarium, meeting rooms, offices, and restrooms. During some events, music can be heard coming from the Interpretive Center's carillon bell tower. The courtyard, large pond, and lawns around the Interpretive Center provide additional resting and picnicking spots. Rentals of the facility help support the arboretum's collections and educational programming.

The arboretum's mission is "to inspire people of all ages to discover and connect with nature through a diverse collection of trees and shrubs hardy to the Inland Northwest" *(the Yakima Area Arboretum website, 2014).* Community education and involvement are vital to the arboretum's operation. A variety of events are offered throughout the year, including the annual Luminaria when visitors take a candlelit walk through the arboretum, an Arbor Day Festival known to be one of the largest in the Pacific Northwest, a fall Mushroom Show, and an annual spring plant sale held on Mother's Day weekend, as well as summer day camps and field trips.

The Yakima Area Arboretum is maintained by a cooperative effort of local garden clubs, affiliated member groups such as the Audubon Society and Iris Society, arboretum staff, and volunteers under the direction of the arboretum's Board of Directors. Visitors can get walking maps of the tree collection in the Jewett Interpretive Center. Guided tours for private groups and individuals can be arranged at no charge by calling (509) 248-7337. See the Yakima Area Arboretum website for more information.

DIRECTIONS FROM I-82 (Us 97): Take Exit 34 to Nob Hill Blvd. Go east on Nob Hill Blvd. and turn onto S. 24th St. (at the first stoplight). Make an immediate left onto Arboretum Drive and follow it to the arboretum's parking area.

Display beds soften the landscape around the arboretum's Jewett Interpretive Center. Photo by Colleen Adams-Schuppe.

Yakima Area Arboretum
www.ahtrees.org

Open daily from dawn to dusk, year-round
Dogs on-leash are welcome

- 46 acres
- No admission fee
- Restrooms available
- Small lunchtime picnics are allowed on the arboretum's lawn and benches. Larger groups require reservations.
- GIFT SHOP: Tree House Museum Store, located in the Jewett Interpretive Center
- PLANT SALES: Annual spring plant sale on Mother's Day weekend
- STRUCTURES/FEATURES: Jewett Interpretive Center (carillon bell tower, Heritage of Trees in the Yakima Valley display, courtyard, restrooms, and meeting space), ponds, foot bridges, pagoda, stone lanterns, wisteria-covered arbors, nature observatory, gazebo, fountain, memorial benches, nursery, and caretaker's cottage
- FEATURED PLANTS/COLLECTIONS: Native trees, crabapples and other fruit trees, nut trees, hawthorns, beeches, sequoias, conifers, maple and oak groves, drought-tolerant plants, roses, lavender, daisies, irises, ornamental grasses, viburnums
- ACTIVITIES: Annual Luminaria event, annual Arbor Day Festival, June Garden Tour, summer Nature Day Camps, field trips (offered year-round), classes on horticulture topics and seasonal crafts, birdwatching workshops
- TOURS: Self-guided tours are welcome. Private, group tours can be arranged by calling (509) 248-7337.
- NEARBY ATTRACTIONS: Downtown Yakima, the Yakima River, the Yakima Greenway (a 10-mile trail that passes through the arboretum's natural area, *www.yakimagreenway.org)*, Yakima Valley Museum, wineries, orchards, and produce stands
- NEARBY GARDENS: Hillside Desert Botanical Gardens (*www.hdbgi. com)*

Display beds, lawns, and numerous trees create a picturesque backdrop for the reflecting pond and gazebo at Lawson Gardens.

29 Lawson Gardens

"Pullman's premier formal garden complex"

Located in a residential area in Southeastern Washington, about 90 minutes south of Spokane on I-95

705 Derby St.
Pullman, WA 99163
(509) 338-3228
www.pullman-wa.gov

Lawson Gardens is a charming, 13-acre formal garden in southeastern Washington. Benches by the *Reflecting Pond* (pictured above) and along the lawns offer quiet places to picnic and relax. Visitors can also stroll by the display beds to observe annuals, perennials, roses, drought-tolerant plants, and trees that are best suited for the region's dry climate.

The idea for the garden began with a local farmer named Gerald Lawson, who donated land for the city to develop a public garden in memory of his first wife, Alice. Mr. Lawson set up an endowment to fund the garden without tax money, and he oversaw every aspect of the garden's initial development. Mr. Lawson worked closely with city officials and a landscape architect to create a master plan for the garden's design and use.

The continued development of Lawson Gardens has been a collaborative effort between the City of Pullman and donors from the community. In 1991, the circular *Rotary Rose Garden* was installed with 600 rose bushes purchased by funds from the Pullman Rotary Club. A *Perennial Garden* was also added to showcase plants of similar color, along with a bed for shade-loving perennials such as hostas, epimediums, and persicarias. North of the Rose Garden, a *Xeric Demonstration Garden* (pictured below), planted by the City of Pullman, showcases a wide variety of bulbs, grasses, perennials, and shrubs using xeriscape techniques to reduce water consumption. Hawthorns, spring flurry serviceberries, western larch, Russian olive, Chinese fringe, and other trees provide a range of color, texture, and shade. A tri-color beech, added to the garden over 25 years ago, is a colorful specimen whose leaves become dark purple as summer approaches.

The Xeric Demonstration Garden displays ornamental grasses, perennials, and shrubs that do well in Eastern Washington's climate. A brochure of plants suitable for xeriscaping can be found on the Lawson Gardens website.

Lawson Gardens is rich with vividly-colored flowers and beds that display plants by color scheme.

The gardens master plan guides improvements or any new display beds that are added. The *Rotary Rose Garden* is one such example. Tea roses planted at the garden's inception proved not to be hardy for the climate, so the garden's horticulturist has gradually replaced them with David Austin English roses. The garden now features roses that can survive the cold winters and hot summers of the region. Good plant choice and mulching help reduce the garden's weeds and water usage. The city is continually improving and expanding the garden. Plans are also being made to add more ponds, a tea house, lookout, and additional theme gardens connected by paths. A conceptual map of the master plan can be found on the garden's website.

Lawson Gardens is located in a quiet community and is commonly used by local residents for leisure activities such as picnicking, photography, painting, reading, and meditating. The gazebo by the central pond can be reserved for weddings. Neither sport-related activities nor pets, other than service animals, are permitted at Lawson Gardens, but they are allowed in the nearby Kruegel Park. Picnic pavilions and restrooms are also available at Kruegel Park. Restrictions might apply. Visit *www.pullman-wa.gov* for more information about Lawson Gardens and the City of Pullman's parks.

Lawson Gardens

www.pullman-wa.gov

Open daily from dawn to dusk, year-round

- 13 acres
- No admission fee
- Picnicking permitted
- Restrooms available at Kruegel Park, across Derby Street
- STRUCTURES/FEATURES: Gazebo, reflecting pond, terraced gardens connected by paths, benches, open lawns shaded by trees
- FUTURE ADDITIONS BEING PLANNED: Ponds, a teahouse, a lookout, and additional theme gardens connected by paths
- FEATURED PLANTS/COLLECTIONS: Epimediums, shade-loving and sun-loving perennials, bulbs, roses, ornamental grasses, drought-tolerant plants, annuals, perennials, a variety of deciduous trees (tri-color beech, Russian olive, crabapple, Chinese fringe, serviceberries, hawthorn)
- ACTIVITIES: Observing combinations and color schemes of plants well-suited for dry climates, hot summers, and cold winters; leisure activities such as reading, painting, photography, picnicking, and meditating. The gazebo can be reserved. Contact the Pullman Parks and Recreation office at (509) 338-3228 for rental information.
- TOURS: Self-guided visits only
- NEARBY ATTRACTIONS: Washington State University-Pullman campus, downtown Pullman, Fine Arts Center, Reaney Park (summer concerts), Kruegel Park, Sunnyside Park (4th of July celebration, nature trails, athletic fields, and picnic shelters)

DIRECTIONS FROM I-95 SOUTHBOUND: Take I-95 south to SR 270 (Davis Way) toward Pullman. Bear left to stay on 270 S., which becomes SE Paradise St. Turn right onto E. Daniel St., then take the first right onto SE Spring St. and left onto Derby St. Watch for the garden's entrance sign.

FROM I-95 NORTHBOUND: Take the SR 27 (S. Grand Avenue) Exit. Turn right onto Crestview St., then left onto SE Spring St. and right onto Derby St. Watch for the garden's entrance sign.

The symmetrical design of the impressive Duncan Gardens in Manito park is anchored by a granite fountain.

30 Manito Park & Gardens
"The crown jewel of Spokane city parks"

Located in Spokane's South Hill area

4 West 21st Avenue
Spokane, WA 99203
(509) 625-6200
https://my.spokanecity.org
www.thefriendsofmanito.org

Spokane's 90-acre Manito Park was established on land that was donated to the City of Spokane in 1904. The acreage was originally used recreationally, with picnic areas, flower beds, and a zoo. The zoo was later removed, and the park now contains 20 acres of five world-class botanical gardens, smaller display beds, and a conservatory.

The parks' three-acre *Duncan Garden* was designed in 1912 by the park's second superintendent, John Duncan, in a classical European Renaissance style (pictured on previous page). Beds of colorful annuals, topiary shrubs, gravel paths, and a hedge border create geometric patterns on opposite sides of the garden's central fountain. The gazebo on the far end of the garden was installed for Manito Park's centennial.

Near Manito Park's historic 1930 stone bridge along the park's scenic *Loop Drive*, clusters of rose beds planted on a knoll make up the award-winning *Rose Hill* (pictured below). The beds were installed in the 1940s by the Spokane Rose Society and Spokane Parks and Recreation. They display 150 varieties of hybrid roses including tea roses, grandiflora, floribunda, miniature roses, and a collection of old-fashioned roses. A pergola was added for the park's centennial. In 2007, Rose Hill was ranked the number one "Outstanding Display Garden" in the U.S. out of 125 All-American Rose Selection gardens.

More than 300 species of perennials, including flowers, small trees, and ornamental grasses, are displayed in the park's *Ferris Perennial Garden*. The Perennial Garden was installed in 1940 and named in honor of a former park board member. Its flowers provide color from spring to fall.

The park's *Lilac Garden* began with lilac cultivars from Rochester, New York and now showcases over 100 lilacs from more than 23 species. An extension was added to the Lilac Garden in 2003 with a contribution from the Spokane Lilac

Manito Park's Rose Hill was ranked the #1 Outstanding Display Garden in the U.S. in 2007.

Society. The lilacs bloom for a short season, creating an impressive display from May to June. The abundance of lilacs planted around the city, including those at Manito Park, are celebrated every May in Spokane's Lilac Festival.

The park's *Nishinomiya Tsutakawa Japanese Garden* is located at the corner of 21st Avenue and Bernard Street, west of the conservatory. It can also be accessed by a path adjacent to Rose Hill. The Japanese Garden was designed by landscape architect Nagao Sakurai and named for both Spokane's sister city and Ed Tsutakawa, who founded the friendship between the two cities. The garden opened in 1974 and features a Japanese-style footbridge spanning a tranquil pond, waterfall, stone lanterns, stone pagoda, flowering cherry trees, Japanese maples, a variety of other plants, and sculptures.

Additional, smaller beds in the garden complex include an *experimental dahlia and iris garden, hardy fuchsia bed,* and *shade garden*. Central to the complex is the *Gaiser Conservatory* (pictured above), named after David Gaiser, park board member and park supporter. Originally built in 1912 and remodeled over the years, it is another one of the remaining glasshouses on the West Coast that can be described as Victorian-style. The conservatory covers 3,546 square feet and is filled with beautiful, flowering displays that change seasonally and can be viewed every day of the year. Its central, curved dome features a waterfall, pond, and tropical plants. Every December, 30,000 holiday lights create a delightful, 10-day show inside the building. The 12,000-square-foot, glass-paned structure comprises both the conservatory and its greenhouses. Admission to the conservatory is free, but donations are gladly accepted.

The gardens at Manito Park are operated by Spokane Parks and Recreation, supported in part by the Friends of Manito. The Friends organization holds plant sales in June and September to benefit the gardens and park improvement projects, and it hosts a gardening lecture series in the park every year. The Children's Renaissance Faire, concerts, and other events are held at the park in summer. The park's Loop Drive offers majestic views of Rose Hill, Mirror Pond, and the Ferris Perennial Garden. *Mirror Pond* is a favorite spot for watching waterfowl and is only a short walk from the gardens. The park also has a seasonal outdoor cafe, picnic areas, grass lawns, ball fields, tennis courts, a playground, splash pad, and a basalt rock office building. Parking is available at several locations, but the closest parking to access the gardens is off 21st Avenue. A walking map and additional information can be found on the Friends of Manito website.

The topiary arches, gazebo, and fountain in Duncan Garden

Manito Park & Gardens
my.spokanecity.org   www.thefriendsofmanito.org

Open daily from dawn to dusk, year-round
(The conservatory has shorter hours November to March)
Dogs on-leash are welcome

- 20 acres of gardens in a 90-acre city park
- No admission fee, but donations are accepted in the conservatory
- Picnicking permitted. Picnic shelters can be reserved.
- Restrooms available
- PLANT SALES: Spring and fall plant sale held by the Friends of Manito
- STRUCTURES/FEATURES: Gaiser Conservatory; pergola and sundial on Rose Hill; granite fountain, gazebo, topiary, display beds in Duncan Gardens; koi pond, foot bridge, waterfall, stone lanterns, stone pagoda, and pavilion in the Japanese Garden; 1930s stone bridge along the park's Loop Drive; Mirror Pond, The Park Bench outdoor cafe, 1912 basalt rock office building, playgrounds, walking trails
- FEATURED PLANTS/COLLECTIONS: Topiary, colorful perennials and annuals, roses, lilacs, dahlias, irises, tropical plants
- ACTIVITES: Annual Holiday Lights display in the Gaiser Conservatory, Children's Renaissance Faire, summer concerts, educational programs, gardening lectures, Spokane Lilac Festival
- TOURS: Self-guided tours only
- NEARBY ATTRACTIONS: Spokane Riverfront Park (cable ride, historic clock tower, trails), John Finch Arboretum
- NEARBY GARDENS: Moore-Turner Heritage Gardens (operated by the City of Spokane, *www.heritagegardens.org*)

*DIRECTIONS FROM I-90 (US 2) EASTBOUND: Take Exit 280 at Maple/ Lincoln. At the second light, turn left. Turn right onto 3rd Ave., then right onto Stevens St. Bear right onto Bernard St. Go up the hill, then turn left onto W. 21st Ave. Watch for the signs to the garden complex. FROM I-90 WESTBOUND: Take Exit 202B onto 2nd Ave. Stay in the left lane. Turn left onto Stevens St. (which becomes Bernard St.). Turn left onto 21st St. and look for the sign at the junction of 21 St. and Park Dr. *For an alternate route from Stevens St., bear left onto W. 9th Ave./S. Grand Blvd. and go up the hill to Manito Park.*

Glossary

The following definitions are from <u>The New Expert</u> by Dr. D.G. Hessayon (1999), the Merriam-Webster Dictionary Online (www.merriam-webster.com), and Wikipedia (www. wikipedia.org).

Annuals—plants that have only one growing season

Arboreta—plural form of the word "arboretum," a place where trees and plants are grown to be studied and/or seen by the public

Champion tree—the largest recorded living specimen of a tree variety in the state

Cultivar—a variety of a plant species that has been cultivated by humans, rather than naturally occurring

Deciduous—plants that lose their leaves at the end of the growing season (not evergreen)

Garden docents—volunteers who lead tours and are knowledgeable about the gardens

Ephemerals—short-blooming, spring flowers

Ericas—plants in the Ericaceae family (i.e. heaths, heathers, rhododendrons, azaleas, and some berries)

Evergreens—plants whose foliage stays green and remains on the plant year-round (not deciduous)

Genus—a group of plants that have one or more species (written in *italics*)

Hardy plants—plants that can withstand frost or overwintering without needing protection

Herbaceous—plants that do not have woody stems

Perennials—plants that have more than one growing season and come back year after year

Pervious—porous, or permeable, material that water can pass through to reduce polluted runoff

Propagate—to produce more of the same type of plant

Species—plants that breed true-to-type from seeds; a genus can have numerous species (for example, there are more than 1,000 *Rhododendron* species)

Variety—a naturally-occurring variation of a species

References

Albers, John J. 2013. *Gardening for Sustainability: Albers Vista Gardens of Kitsap.* Bremerton, WA: Vista Gardens Press.

Dietz, Duane. "Talking to the Rocks: The Garden of Ione and Emmott Chase." *Pacific Horticulture.* Spring 1998.

Graves, Greg. "Compost Happens: Redeeming Disaster." *Pacific Horticulture. Vol. 73, No. 4, pp. 42-45.* Fall 2012.

Hessayon, Dr. D.G. 1999. *The New Flower Expert.* London: Expert Books.

Hinckley, Thomas M. "The University of Washington and The College of Forest Resources' Center for Urban Horticulture: History and Programs." *Landscape Planning and Horticulture, abstract, Vol. 2, No. 2.*

Lakewold Gardens. *Garden Lovers Guide to the Pacific NW (featuring select Northwest gardens and estates).*

Lykins, Craig and Fleming, Michael. 2001. *A Garden in Four Seasons: The Carl S. English, Jr. Botanical Garden at Hiram M. Chittenden Locks.* Seattle, WA: Northwest Interpretive Association.

Short, Mike. 2004. *Ohme Gardens Alpine Wonderland: Making The Dream a Reality.* Wenatchee, WA: Cascade Graphics and Printing, Inc.

Wingate, Mary. 2007. *The Bellevue Botanical Garden: Celebrating the First 15 Years.* Bellevue, WA: Garden Bench Books.

Online Resources

"100 Years and Beyond: A Brief History of Point Defiance Park." *The News Tribune.* www.thepark.thenewstribune. com/history

Better Homes and Garden. www.bhg.com/gardening/plant-dictionary

Easton, Valerie. "Soos Creek Botanical Garden Welcomes You." *Seattle Times: Pacific NW Magazine.* www.seattle times.com/pacific-nw-magazine. Published August 12, 2011.

Easton, Valerie. "A Northwest Holiday Wonderland is Woven from Treasured Collections on a Farm in Orting." *Seattle Times: Pacific NW Magazine*. www.seattletimes.com/pacific-nw-magazine. Published December 14, 2008.

Form and Foliage. "South Seattle Community College Arboretum: A Hidden Gem of a Conifer Garden." www.formandfoliage.wordpress.com. October 6, 2013.

Funderburg, Lise. "The Thrill of the Chases." *Garden Design*. www.gardendesign.com. February-March 2013.

Garden Conservancy Northwest Network. www.garden conservancynorthwestnetwork.org

Gardens for Peace. www.gardensforpeace.org

Great Plant Picks. www.greatplantpicks.org

Hardy Fern Foundation. www.hardyferns.org

Hiltz, Jackie. "A Life's Masterpiece at Soos Creek Botanical Garden." *Crosscut: News of the Great Nearby*. www.cross cut.com. August 17, 2012.

Kidd, Sue. "Common Ground" (a story about Point Defiance Park's history). *The News Tribune*. www.thenewstribune.com/2005/06/01/29104/common-ground. June 1, 2005

Northwest Horticulture Society. www.northwesthort.org.

Pacific Horticulture. www.pacifichorticulture.org/articles-highline-seatac-botanical-garden

Royal Horticulture Society. www.rhs.org.uk

Stahl, Dean. "Chase Garden: A Growing Legacy." *Seattle Times: Pacific NW Magazine*. www.commnity.seattletimes.nwsource.com/archive. May 14, 1995.

The Plant List. www.theplantlist.org.

West Seattle Blog. http://westseattleblog.com/2010/10/south-Seattle-community-college-now-has-a-peace-garden/

Whitney, Michael. "Arboretum Celebrates 50 Years in Everett." *Tribune: Snohomish County News*. www.snoho.com/stories_2013/040314_arboretum. April 3, 2013.

*The majority of the gardens in this book are tagged on Google maps at *www.google.com/maps (also www.google maps.com)*. Type the garden name or address in the search box to get driving directions.

Local Interest Websites

City of Auburn. www.auburnwa.gov
City of Bellevue parks. www.ci.bellevue.wa.us
City of Everett. www.ci.everett.wa.us
City of Lakewood. www.cityoflakewood.us
City of Olympia (state capitol). www.olympia.wa.gov
City of Woodland. www.ci.woodland.wa.us
City of Yakima. www.yakimawa.gov
Downtown Seattle. www.downtownseattle.com
Experience Washington. www.experiencewa.com
Frommers (free, interactive maps). www.frommers.com
Leavenworth. www.leavenworth.org
Metro Parks Tacoma. www.metroparkstacoma.org
National Park Service. www.nps.gov/state/wa
Pullman Chamber of Commerce. www.pullmanchamber.com
Scenic Washington State (scenic byways). www.scenicwa.com
Seattle and Sound: Things to Do in Seattle and the Entire
Puget Sound Region. www.seattleandsound.com
Seattle government and tourism. www.seattle.gov/visiting
Travel Tacoma. www.traveltacoma.com
Visit Kitsap Peninsula. www.visitkitsap.com
Visit Seattle. www.visitseattle.com
Visit Spokane. www.visitspokane.com
Visit Yakima. www.visityakima.com
Wenatchee. www.wenatchee.org
Whidbey Camano Islands. www.whidbeycamanoislands.com
Yakima Greenway Foundation. www.yakimagreenway.org
Yakima Valley. www.visityakima.com

*If traveling I-90 through the Cascade Mountains, you might
encounter delays due to rock blasting and construction for the
Snoqualmie Pass East "wildlife corridor project." Information
on blasting times and potential delays is available at www.
wsdot.wa.gov (under the I-90 Snoqualmie Pass East link) and
www.conservationnw.org (including a video, rock blasting
times, and information on traffic delays).*